CAPTAIN COOK

C A P T A I N   C O O K

July, 1972, Selection of the YOUNG ADULTS' DIVISION
of the LITERARY GUILD

All orders and correspondence should be addressed to

**DOUBLEDAY & COMPANY, INC.
School and Library Division
Garden City, L.I., New York 11530**

A medallion portrait of James Cook (1728–79) by Josiah
Wedgwood, from a design by John Flaxman, cast in 1784

ALISTAIR MACLEAN

CAPTAIN COOK

Doubleday & Company, Inc.
Garden City, New York.

Contents

In 1775, on his return from his second voyage, the Royal
Society awarded Cook the Copley Gold Medal

Prologue

SHORTLY after the turn of the nineteenth century, a young gunner in the Royal Navy, a certain Jeremy Blyth, who had yet to sail on his first commission, made his way into an ale-house in Wapping. It was a dock-side tavern typical of its time and place, dirty, smoky, with cracked floor-boards and blackened walls and ceiling, entirely lacking in what, even in that era, passed for the more civilised amenities of life. A planked bar, a few rickety tables and chairs; that was all. Typical, too, were the customers: a mixture of seamen from both naval services, many the victims of press-gangs, many with criminal pasts, hard-drinking, hard-swearing, hard-living men inured to suffering and hardships and death, men tough and enduring and hard-bitten to a degree almost incomprehensible to those who live in a gentler and more effete age.

Atypical, however, was the atmosphere in that ale-house. No one spoke. No one drank. The silence was accentuated by occasional sobs. The landlord, shoulders heaving, had his head buried in his forearms. So did a number of those at the tables. Some of the men were openly weeping and all seemed lost in their own private worlds of grief-stricken desolation. Blyth sat down opposite a grizzled old seaman, a grey-cheeked veteran with tears welling from sightless eyes, an untouched drink before him. Wonderingly, gently, Blyth touched him on the forearm.

'What is it? What's wrong?'

The old man looked up from the table and said angrily 'Haven't you heard? Haven't you heard?'

7

Blyth shook his head.

'Nelson is dead.'

Again Blyth looked slowly round the dingy room, at the men for whom the death of Nelson had left an aching void that could never be filled, then he said: 'Thank God I never knew him.'

It is doubtful whether any such scene occurred, or any remotely comparable, when the news of Cook's death reached England some twenty-six years earlier. The nation mourned him, as England has always mourned the passing of its great men, its Marlboroughs, its Wellingtons, its Churchills: but it did not weep with a broken heart.

Nelson and Cook are the two most revered names in the annals of the Royal Navy. Reverence is compounded of respect and love. Nelson was widely respected but universally loved. Cook was universally respected but he was incapable of inspiring in the minds and hearts of the public that degree of devotion and adoration that Nelson so effortlessly and inevitably aroused. But that Cook was beloved by his officers and men is beyond dispute.

The reason for the difference lies, of course, in the natures of the two men. To love a person, a public figure, one has to be able to identify one's self with him: to do that, one has to know him – or, at least, believe that one knows him. In so far as this was concerned, there was no difficulty at all about Nelson, a warm-hearted, outgoing extrovert whose inner thoughts and private life were as open a book as his public ones. But Cook's inner thoughts and private life were a closed book, one of those old-fashioned books with a brass hasp that he'd locked and then thrown away the key. With the passing of the years it seems increasingly unlikely that the key will ever be found.

We know all about Cook and we know nothing about him. We know that he was courageous, prudent, wise, indefatigable, adventurous, a born leader of men: but what he was *like*, what kind of individual he was personally, we have but the most remote of conceptions. We know that he took those leaking old coal-boats of his from the tropical Pacific to the bitter and awesome wastes of both the Arctic and the Antarctic in the most stupendous voyages of exploration in the history of mankind. But whether he liked flowers or dandled his children on his knee or gazed enraptured at the sun going down in the ocean beyond Hawaii or Tahiti we shall never know. We know he was the greatest navigator of his age or any age: it would be interesting to know if he ever got lost in the back streets of his home borough of Stepney.

To have maintained so inviolate a privacy is indeed a feat, but to have done so in spite of the fact that he left us over one million words minutely recording his day to day activities over many years amounts to an accomplishment so staggering as to defy rational comprehension. But, in his journals and logs, this is what Cook did indeed do. No famous figure of modern times has ever documented his life so thoroughly and painstakingly. But this massive documentation is detached, impersonal; Cook does not appear: it was about what he did, not what he was. Even in his private correspondence – what little of it has survived – this same iron reticence manifests itself. Only twice does he mention his wife and then only in an incidental fashion: of his two children who died in infancy or his daughter who died at the age of four, there is no authenticated instance of Cook ever having mentioned them.

His contemporaries wrote of him of course, from Walpole to Dr Johnson they all had their say, and when all their writing is over and done with we learn no more about Cook than we learn from Cook himself. Maybe they did not know him as they would have liked to know him: maybe he was reserved to the point of being unapproachable. It may even have been that they were aware that they were dealing with an already living legend who was destined for immortality. If this were the case then their task was impossible: the myth envelops the man, so cocooning its creator in the folds of his fame that it becomes virtually certain that not even the keenest eye can penetrate to the heart of the legend, a legend that will accept only the most grandiose rhetoric, the most broad and sweeping generalisations: one does not customarily discuss an immortal's taste in cravats or whether he stopped to smell the lilac on an evening late in May.

Biographies of Cook there have been, of course, many of them. But none of them is the good and true and definitive biography of a man about whom we should like to know so much. It is very much to be doubted whether there will ever be such a biography. Most of the biographers who have tried to flesh out the skeleton of his awesome reputation have had to have recourse to varying degrees of invention or imagination while honestly trying to remain within the bounds of probability. Thus, we are told on one occasion that Mrs Cook welcomed her husband home with tearful affection after one of his marathon voyages, affection because he had been so long away, tearful because one of their children had died in his absence. Now, this is very likely: but there is nothing on record to justify such an assertion. She may, for all we know, have hit him over the head with a two-by-four. This, admittedly, is extremely unlikely. The point is that, in the absence of evidence to the contrary, it is not impossible. Extrapolation and uninspired guesses are no substitute for historical accuracy.

It has been said that the definitive biography is only a matter of time. I don't believe it. It has been said that if Cook's million words are subjected to the combined scrutinies of a statistician, an analyst and psychiatrist the truth must out. That something would finally emerge one does not doubt but as the liability of statisticians, analysts and psychiatrists to error is established and notorious the mind boggles at the prospect of such error trebly compounded. *Requiescat in pace*. It is unthinkable that an immortal should be subjected to the processes of computerised butchery.

Far from being intended to be a definitive biography, what follows is no biography at all. A true biography is a fully-rounded portrait but there are colours missing from my palette. I do not know enough about the man: the material just is not there. This is but a brief account of his early apprenticeship to the sea, his development as a navigator and cartographer, and of his three great voyages, and this is perhaps enough to let us have an inkling of the essential Captain Cook for he was a man, as he himself confessed, to whom achievement meant all. In his last letter written to Lord Sandwich from Capetown in 1776 he said: 'My endeavour shall not be wanting to achieve the great object of this voyage'. It never was. It was not what Cook said or thought that raised him to the ranks of the immortals: it was what he did.

Let the deeds speak for the man.

London's famous statue of Captain James Cook near Admiralty Arch

CHAPTER I

THE ABLE SEAMAN

JAMES COOK, who was to become a Post-Captain in the Royal Navy and the greatest combination of seaman, explorer, navigator and cartographer that the world has known, was born in 1728 of obscure parents in an obscure village in Yorkshire. His mother was a local girl, his father a Scot, a farm labourer. There has been considerable speculation as to which parent transmitted the seeds of genius to Cook, a speculation as singularly pointless as it is totally inconclusive as we know nothing of either of them.

After a sporadic education and a few years' work on his father's employer's farm, Cook left home at the age of seventeen for the tiny seaport of Staithes. This move has been cited as the first stirrings of that restless and soaring ambition that was to take Cook to the uttermost ends of the earth. It may equally well have been that he was just fed up with the farm for it seems unlikely that a boy suffused with dreams of glory would have gone to work in a grocer's and haberdasher's shop, which is what Cook did.

The prospect of a lifetime behind a counter clearly appealed to Cook no more than the prospect of one behind a plough for in 1746, at the age of eighteen, he left the haberdashery trade, a life to which he was never to return, and betook himself to the sea, which was to be his home, his life and his consuming passion until his death thirty-three years later.

He was apprenticed to John and Henry Walker, shipowners, of Whitby, who specialised in the colliery trade. The ships employed for this purpose were, as one might imagine,

Whitby harbour in about 1820. It was here in Whitby that Cook
served his apprenticeship

singularly unlovely, broad-beamed and bulky, much given
to wallowing in a sickening fashion in any condition short
of perfect, and notoriously poor and slow and difficult
sailors under all conditions. But to the owners of eighteenth-
century colliers aesthetics were irrelevant, pragmatism was
all: such vessels were designed solely to carry large quantities
of coal in bulk and for this task they were superbly equipped.

But they were possessed of other and unlikely qualities.
Despite the fact that they were designed and built along the
lines of a cross between a Dutch clog and a coffin they had remarkable sea-keeping qualities and could ride out the most
violent of gales although, admittedly, to the vast discomfort
of their unfortunate crews. Their flat-bottomed design

permitted them to be hauled ashore on suitably sandy beaches for careening. And, of course, they were capable of carrying vast quantities of provisions. So perhaps it was not after all so ludicrous that it was to be those lumbering Whitby colliers and not the Navy's dashing frigates and cruisers that were to take Cook to the furthest ends of the earth.

Cook, then, served aboard such a vessel – the *Freelove*, a 450-tonner – for the first two seasons of his apprenticeship, plying the coal route between Newcastle and London, before transferring to another Walker vessel, the *Three Brothers*, which extended the limits of his geographical knowledge and seamanship by taking him to the west coast of England, to Ireland and to Norway.

Little is known of Cook's professional or social life during this period. Indeed, he doesn't appear to have had any social life whatsoever for between voyages or when vessels were laid up for the winter Cook devoted himself exclusively to the pursuit not of pleasure but of learning. This is one of the few facts of his early life that can be established without difficulty, for the Walkers – with whom Cook stayed when not at sea – and their friends were moved to record their astonishment at the long hours Cook spent in improving his knowledge of navigation, astronomy and mathematics. This was a habit that Cook was never to lose: he kept learning until he died.

His apprenticeship over, Cook left the Walkers, spent over two years in the East Coast and Baltic trade, then was asked by the Walker brothers to return to them and become mate of their vessel the *Friendship*. Cook accepted. Three years later, in 1755, he was offered the command of the *Friendship*. Cook declined. Instead, he joined the Royal Navy as an able seaman.

This extraordinary decision does two things: it points up a fact and raises a question. The fact is that, to have been offered a command at the age of twenty-seven, Cook must

A first rate off the Deptford docks as another is prepared for
launching

have impressed the owners with his qualities as a seaman, a
navigator and a leader of men, which is perhaps not surprising
when one considers the quite extraordinary lengths to which
he was going to develop those already marked abilities – and
that of the practice of cartography – in the years to come.
But what is surprising is that he passed up the command of
a merchant ship for the lowest rank of a naval vessel.

As with so many of his decisions, Cook himself has offered
no explanation for this one. (Cook was an intensely secretive
man – in his wanderings over the world his officers frequently
complained that they never knew where they were going
until they got there.) It is generally assumed that it was
directly connected with the frantic re-arming taking place
in Britain and France in preparation for the inevitable approach of what, the following year, was to be the beginning
of the bitter and bloody Seven Years' War: active fighting
was already taking place in overseas territories, especially in
North America, where Britain and France had already

abandoned all pretence of diplomatic negotiations as a means of settling the question of colonial supremacy: already, although it was still nominally peace-time, the British Navy had instituted a tight blockade of the French coast to prevent further supplies of men and arms from reaching the French in Canada.

Because of a Navy that had been allowed to become run-down and depleted and because of the imminence of war, British shipyards were turning out naval vessels at an unprecedented rate. Ships need crews and the young men of that day and age were markedly reluctant to volunteer for this honour, an unwillingness that is no cause for surprise when one considers the brutal conditions of life in the Royal Navy of the mid-eighteenth century. They had to be persuaded to man those empty vessels and as recruiting posters weren't very much in vogue at that time persuasion usually took the form of forcible abduction, by heavily-armed naval press-gangs, of any able-bodied man, drunk or sober, who was so unfortunate as to cross their path. It has been suggested that Cook volunteered so as to avoid being press-ganged, but, apart from the fact that it seems totally out of character with the man, it is incredible that a merchant navy officer – and Cook could have been a captain, had he so wished – would have been press-ganged without being released, with apologies, the moment his identity was known.

Perhaps he was a romantic who could hear the far-off sound of drums and bugles. Perhaps his patriotism was of less euphoric nature, a combination of conscience and common-sense that told him it was not only his duty but also prudent to smite the French before they smote him. Perhaps – this is the most commonly suggested explanation and an uncommonly cynical one it is too – Cook figured that with so many ships being built and with the certainty of so many men being killed in the now inevitable war, promotion was bound to be rapid. Perhaps he was just tired of the eternal coal dust. Perhaps anything. We shall never know. All that we know with certainty is that he joined the Navy on 17 June 1755, and eight days later was assigned to the *Eagle*, a sixty-gun ship of the line lying at Portsmouth.

The *Eagle* in turn was assigned to the blockade of the French coast. As he was from then on to do faithfully for the rest of his life, Cook kept a day-to-day log, but it makes for rather less than dramatic and inspirational reading. He mentions such things as watch changes, conditions of the food and drink, gives us weather reports, speaks of patrols, sighting and investigating ships, hum-drum details which after two centuries can hold no interest for us because, as ever, they tell us nothing of the man himself.

Only two things of any note occurred in his first few months on the *Eagle*. Within a month of joining, he had become master's mate, indication enough of the speed with which his navigational ability, seamanship and reliability had been appreciated. Then, not long afterwards, the *Eagle's* captain, an easy-going gentleman who vastly preferred the sheltered calms of Portsmouth harbour to the winter gales of the English Channel, was relieved of his command and replaced by Captain (later Sir) Hugh Palliser.

Palliser, as he was to prove, was no ordinary man. A brilliant seaman and naval tactician, held in the highest regard by his superiors, he was eventually to become Governor of Newfoundland and a Lord of the Admiralty. Even so, he might have been entirely forgotten today, his tiny niche in history obliterated by Cook's great shadow, were it not for the fact that it was Palliser who first recognised Cook as a man of genius and destiny, who proclaimed this loud and long to all in authority who would listen and who, as his years drew in, long after Cook's place in history was assured, was still happily proclaiming his belief in Cook's destiny. Palliser must have been a man of quite extraordinary perception.

Cook remained on the *Eagle* from the summer of 1755

Sir Hugh Palliser, the first to recognize Cook's genius and one of his most influential admirers (Nathaniel Dance)

until the autumn of 1757 – the Seven Years' War had begun early in 1756, but the declaration of war did no more than regularise an already existing situation. Except for occasional urgent refits – the weather in the Channel and the Bay of Biscay caused far more damage to the English men-o'-war than the French did – the *Eagle* spent almost all of this time blockading the French coast. It was a rather hum-drum and monotonous existence enlivened only by the first – and last – sea-fight of any importance in which Cook was to engage. In late May, 1757, they engaged a large French vessel, 1500 tons and fifty guns, off Ushant – an East Indiaman by the name of *Duc d'Aquitaine*. The French vessel, in a running fight lasting forty minutes, was crippled and captured: but the *Eagle* itself was so badly damaged that it had to return to England for repairs.

For our understanding of Cook, the significance of this period lies not in the occasional skirmishes with the enemy but in the fact that it was then that Cook polished and honed the skills, those very special skills, that were to serve him so well in the years to come. True, he was still no cartographer, his years of surveying and chart-work were yet to come: but that he had fully mastered his knowledge of ships and the sea is shown clearly by the fact that in just over two years he had advanced from able seaman to master's mate, to boatswain and finally to master, the person in charge of the actual running of the ship and the senior non-commissioned officer on board. At the same time, he pursued his studies in navigation and mathematics (in necessary conjunction with astronomy) and as he had already been fully qualified in those subjects before he had joined the Navy the standards he had now reached must have been quite exceptional.

The mastering of those subjects was, of course, an essential prerequiste for the years in the Pacific that still lay far ahead – without them he could never have gone and the Admiralty would most certainly never have chosen him. But no less essential for the future was his exposure and conditioning to naval life itself, so different from the careless and rather slipshod way of life found aboard the colliers. Here each man was a specialist, a man trained to rely upon himself and to rely upon others, a man into whose mind it was firmly and permanently inculcated that he was a vital link in a chain and that the one unforgiveable sin, under times of stress – and Cook and his men were to undergo a much greater degree of stress in the Pacific than they had ever been subjected to in the Atlantic – was to be the one who broke that chain. Much has rightly been said about the harshness of naval discipline at the time, but overmuch misplaced emphasis has been laid on the contention that only an iron discipline could produce a highly trained crew. Only bad crews, badly officered, require this brutal kind of discipline, while good crews, good officers, all highly trained, need only the discipline that comes from within: it is clear, now and later, that this was the kind of crew Cook had in mind.

On 27 October 1757, Cook joined the *Pembroke*, a sixty-four gun ship, as master. It was his twenty-ninth birthday. For most of the winter his new ship carried out the blockade in the Bay of Biscay. In February, 1758, they sailed for Canada.

The war was going badly for the British on the North American continent. General Braddock's army had been savagely handled by the French and Indians and it was considered imperative and of the utmost urgency to take the pressure off the British colonial forces in what is now the eastern seaboard of the United States by launching an attack against the French in the north, the main objective being the centre of their military power, Quebec.

There is no evidence that Cook took any active part in the first part of this operation which consisted in the reduction of the powerful fortress of Louisburg which guarded the gateway to the St Lawrence. This fortress fell to General Wolfe,

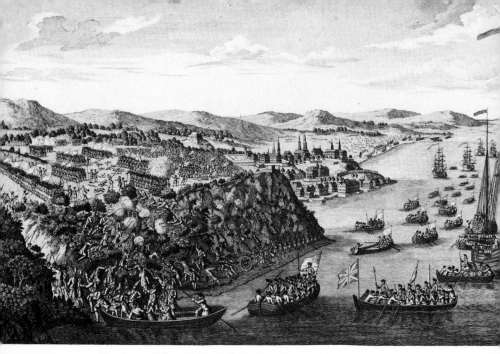

A view of the taking of Quebec (September 1759)

who was to die the following year in the taking of Quebec, after bitter fighting and a lengthy siege. But Cook had a role to play in the Quebec campaign itself, not a major one, perhaps, but one which was essential for the success of the operation.

This took place some ten months after the surrender of Louisburg: Wolfe's army, though victorious, had been badly mauled and had to await reinforcements from England while the Navy was glad of the opportunity to refit its ships during the winter at Halifax. But by May of 1759, advance units of the British forces had penetrated up the St Lawrence to within a few miles of Quebec.

Here they encountered a major but expected difficulty. Navigation on the river at this point becomes difficult to a degree. Up to this point normal deep-water traffic follows the northern shore, then switches across river to the south to approach the basin of Quebec itself. The stretch of water where the crossing is made is known as the Traverse and as far as river navigational hazards are concerned it can have few equals in the world: it is a confusing and highly treacherous maze of rocks and shoals and shifting sandbars, a navigator's nightmare if ever there was one. If, that is to say, the channel through the Traverse is not accurately buoyed.

On this occasion, May 1759, it wasn't. It had been, but the French, understandably enough, had removed every last buoy. It fell to the lot of Cook and the masters of one or two other vessels to re-chart and re-buoy the passage, a difficult and arduous task lasting several weeks, a task that was made no easier by the fact that Cook and the others worked mostly under the range of French guns, that they had to work frequently at night and that the French had the infuriating habit of coming out from shore in canoes during the hours of darkness and cutting away buoys which had to be replaced

The Newfoundland coastline charted by Cook and others

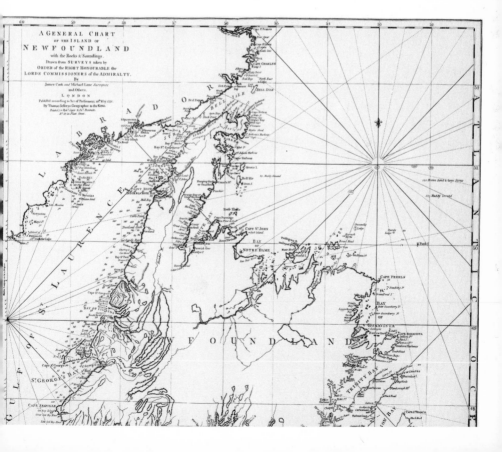

the next day – after, that is, fresh soundings had been taken.

But by June all was ready and in that month the entire British armada of over two hundred ships safely made the passage of the Traverse without a single casualty. There is little question that the bulk of the credit belonged to Cook: in official despatches he was now being referred to as 'Master Surveyor'. As a mark of the esteem in which he was already held it may be mentioned that Wolfe consulted him about the placement of several ships before Quebec – a general seeking the advice of a man who wasn't even an officer. But Wolfe, doubtless, recognised an expert when he saw one.

After the siege and capture of Quebec – Cook took no physical part in any of this – most of the naval vessels were sent home for a refit, including the *Pembroke*, but Cook had to wait another three years before he saw England again for he was transferred to the *Northumberland*, flagship of the commander-in-chief, Lord Colville – a certain indication that he was now regarded as the ablest master in the fleet.

For the next three years, at the personal request of Admiral Colville, Cook continued to chart, firstly, the St Lawrence and then the coast of Newfoundland. That he was eminently successful in the execution of his duties is clear from three things. In January 1761, Lord Colville directed the storekeeper 'to pay the master of the *Northumberland* fifty pounds in consideration of his indefatigable industry in making himself master of the pilotage of the River Saint Lawrence'. The following year Admiral Colville sent Cook's charts home to the Admiralty urging that they should publish them and adding: 'From my experience of Mr Cook's genius and capacity I think him well qualified for the work he has performed and for greater undertakings of the same kind' – a prophetic opinion if ever there was one. Finally, Cook's charts appeared in the *North American Pilot* in 1775 and were to remain the standard works of navigational reference for those waters for over a century.

Table Mountain at The Cape, painted by Hodges

A painting by William Hodges of the *Resolution* and *Adventure* at anchor in Matavai Bay, Tahiti

This kangaroo was painted by George Stubbs from a skin brought back to England by Joseph Banks

The Australian dingo observed in the Endeavour River area and thought at first to be a wolf. The painting is by George Stubbs

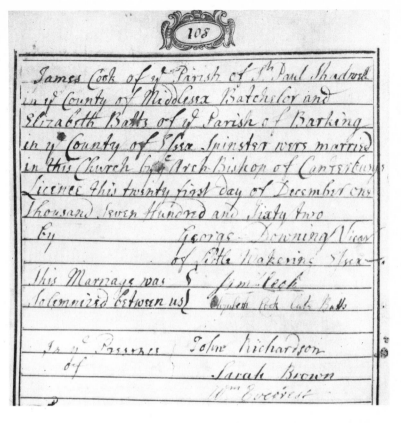

The church registry record of Cook's marriage to Elizabeth Batts. Mrs Cook died in 1835 at the age of 93 (outliving her husband by 56 years). Three of their six children survived infancy but these three died early and tragic deaths, two of them by drowning

Cook returned home in November 1762. In December he married a certain Elizabeth Batts. This has been the cause of much eyebrow-raising among historians over the years for whatever else Cook may have been, dashing and impetuous he was not and the thought of this steady, calm and careful man engaging in a whirlwind courtship does not find easy acceptance. On the other hand, to say that Cook wasn't much

A portrait by an unknown artist of Elizabeth Cook in old age

given to talking about himself is to put the matter in a very restrained fashion indeed and for all we know to the contrary he may have known her from the time she could walk. In any event, speculation is pointless for Mrs Cook, regrettably, forms no part of the story of Captain Cook: regrettably, for to have known more about her would have given us a deeper inferential insight into Cook's character. But we know nothing about her, just as we know nothing about any of their children. They remain shadowy and insubstantial figures, people without faces on the far periphery of Captain Cook's life. They are only names.

The next five years of Cook's life were comparatively uneventful, devoted in the main to endless studies and the steady increase of his already vast store of knowledge and experience. In the spring of 1763 he returned to Canada where he spent the summer surveying and charting the east coast: in the winter he returned to England where he spent the next few months working up his charts for publication. This pattern was repeated for the next four years during which he was given the command of his own schooner to help him in his work – a command, be it noted, not a commission.

It is a quite staggering reflection that when Cook left Canada for the last time in 1767, he was still a non-commissioned officer. It is also a staggering reflection on the Lords of the Admiralty of the time that, because of their innate snobbish conviction that officers and gentlemen are born and not made, Cook did not quite qualify for a commission. He had been in the despised Merchant Service, he had sailed before the mast in the Navy, he was poor and his origins were obscure. There could have been little doubt left in the Admiralty by that time that in Cook they had the greatest seaman, navigator and cartographer of the generation. But a commission? Hardly. Hardly, that was, until they realised that to send a naval vessel to circumnavigate the globe, in the greatest exploratory voyage ever undertaken, under the command of a non-commissioned officer wouldn't be quite the thing to do. For one thing, it would redound most dreadfully upon the alleged competence of those who did hold commissions and, for another, it would not look good in the history books. So, belatedly, they made him a lieutenant.

CHAPTER 2

THE VANISHING CONTINENT

THE Lords of the Admiralty made Cook a lieutenant for the excellent reason that he was not only the automatic but the only choice for the task they had in mind. For the task, that is, that they had privately in mind, for the Admiralty, then as now, could be a very devious lot indeed and their publicly announced plans bore little relationship to their true intentions.

Ostensibly, the Admiralty had no direct involvement in the forthcoming voyage. Ostensibly, they were merely and

A late sixteenth-century map of the world showing the unknown continent as it was then conceived

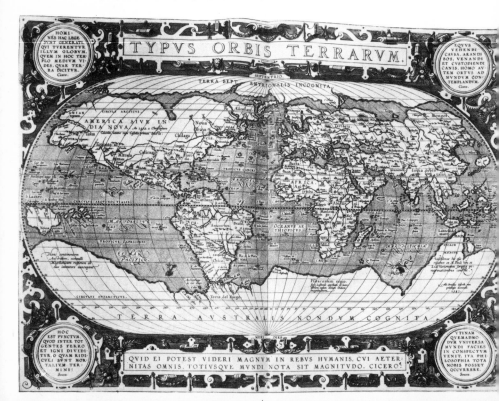

generously providing transport to an as yet undecided destination in the Pacific for a group of astronomers who wished
to observe a transit of Venus – that is, the passage of Venus
between the sun and the earth on 3 June 1769. The astronomers were members of the even then prestigious Royal
Society. There had been a previous transit of Venus in 1762
but the observations achieved had ranged from unsatisfactory
to useless. This observation that the Royal Society now hoped
to make was expected to be of the greatest value in the advance
of astronomical navigation. (The results of 1769 were to turn
out to be no better than those of 1762: unknown to the
astronomers of the day the instruments then available lacked
sufficient delicacy and precision for the task.)

Behind this ostensible reason for the voyage lay the
Admiralty's secondary reason. France was trying to spread
her influence and annex what territories she could in the
Pacific and Britain was determined not to let her have the
field to herself, which, in retrospect, was rather mean of
Britain because it had just driven the French out of both
North America and India and already owned one-eighth of
the known world. But they were an acquisitively-minded
and expansionist people in those days and the more they had
the more they wanted. Already, in pursuance of this land-
grabbing policy, the Admiralty had despatched, in the
previous four years, two expeditions across the Pacific, one
under Commodore Byron, the other under Captain Wallis.
Neither had much luck. As usual, Byron – the famous Foul
Weather Jack – managed to get himself completely lost in
the Pacific, which is, admittedly, no very difficult thing to
do, and arrived home more by good luck than anything else
without having discovered anything. Wallis, an extremely
competent sailor, was beset by vicious weather throughout,
but he did discover Tahiti. The Admiralty had it in mind that
Cook might have better luck.

But behind the Admiralty's secondary reason lay its

Alexander Dalrymple, geographer and member of the
Royal Society, and fanatical believer in the mythical
southern continent

primary reason, which was given to Cook in highly secret
instructions that were known to half of London in a very
short time: those instructions said, in effect, that he was to go
and see if he couldn't find a new continent.

There was, at that time, a widely-held belief that there
existed a very large continent in the southern hemisphere, a
continent that girdled the globe, not an Antarctica, but a
temperate continent that reached up almost to South America
and New Zealand, and that occupied most of the south
Pacific. Some geographers had even drawn fanciful maps of
the region – it has to be remembered that, even just over two

hundred years ago, man's ignorance of those regions was total. The main protagonist of this idea was one Alexander Dalrymple, also, by coincidence, an astronomer of the Royal Society. His belief in this idea was obsessive to the extent that it became the corner-stone of his life: he was never to forgive Cook for destroying his dream.

On the basis of this three-pronged plan, then, it is clear that the Admiralty had no alternative to Cook. To penetrate into the unknown waters beyond the roaring forties where weather conditions such as not experienced anywhere else in the world might well be encountered, called for an outstanding seaman, and this Cook undoubtedly was. It called for a man who always knew where he was – and if Cook with his navigational qualifications didn't know where he was then no one else in the world was very likely to either. It called for a cartographer who could accurately dilineate the coastlines of as yet undiscovered lands and in this capacity Cook had no equal. Finally, and ironically, it called for a man who had the qualifications to command this purportedly Royal Society expedition. Those Cook had also: not only was he a very capable astronomer but he had actually covered a transit for the Royal Society while in Canada.

It is worth noting, in the passing, that Alexander Dalrymple, who appeared to have a certain amount of belief in himself, was of the opinion that *he* should be given command of the expedition, an illusion swiftly and sadly shattered when Sir Edward Hawke, First Lord of the Admiralty, thumped a table and swore that he would sooner lose his right hand than give command of a King's ship to one who had not been bred in the Navy.

That the Navy had, in fact, selected Cook for the command long before they either asked him or made their choice public is quite clear from the fact that the vessel they had already chosen for the expedition was the type of ship that Cook knew best – a Whitby collier. She was a vessel in which,

The *Earl of Pembroke*, later to become famous as the *Endeavour*, leaving Whitby harbour. As a Whitby collier, she was a class of boat that Cook knew very well

today, the more intrepid might venture to sail from Dover to Calais, provided, that is to say, that the weather forecast was good. The *Earl of Pembroke*, as the vessel was then known, was as unimpressive as she was unprepossessing. For the great task ahead she was ludicrously small, with wide bluff bows, a raised poop and a square stern. Her maximum speed with all sails under the best of conditions would be about seven knots.

However, she was very strongly built and, like all Whitby colliers, had remarkable sea-keeping qualities. She was re-named the *The Endeavour Bark* but was never thereafter called anything except *Endeavour*.

The *Endeavour* was very wide in the beam – almost thirty feet which seems a quite extraordinary width for a vessel of just over a hundred feet in length – and she had every need to

A scale model of the *Endeavour*, now in the National Maritime Museum, Greenwich

be. Apart from carrying a complement of close on a hundred souls, room had to be found for an immense amount of stores and equipment. The question of food alone, one would have thought, presented an almost insuperable problem – enough to tide ninety-four men over an estimated minimum period of two years. (The basic elements of the diet were salt pork and biscuits – two commodities to which weevils became

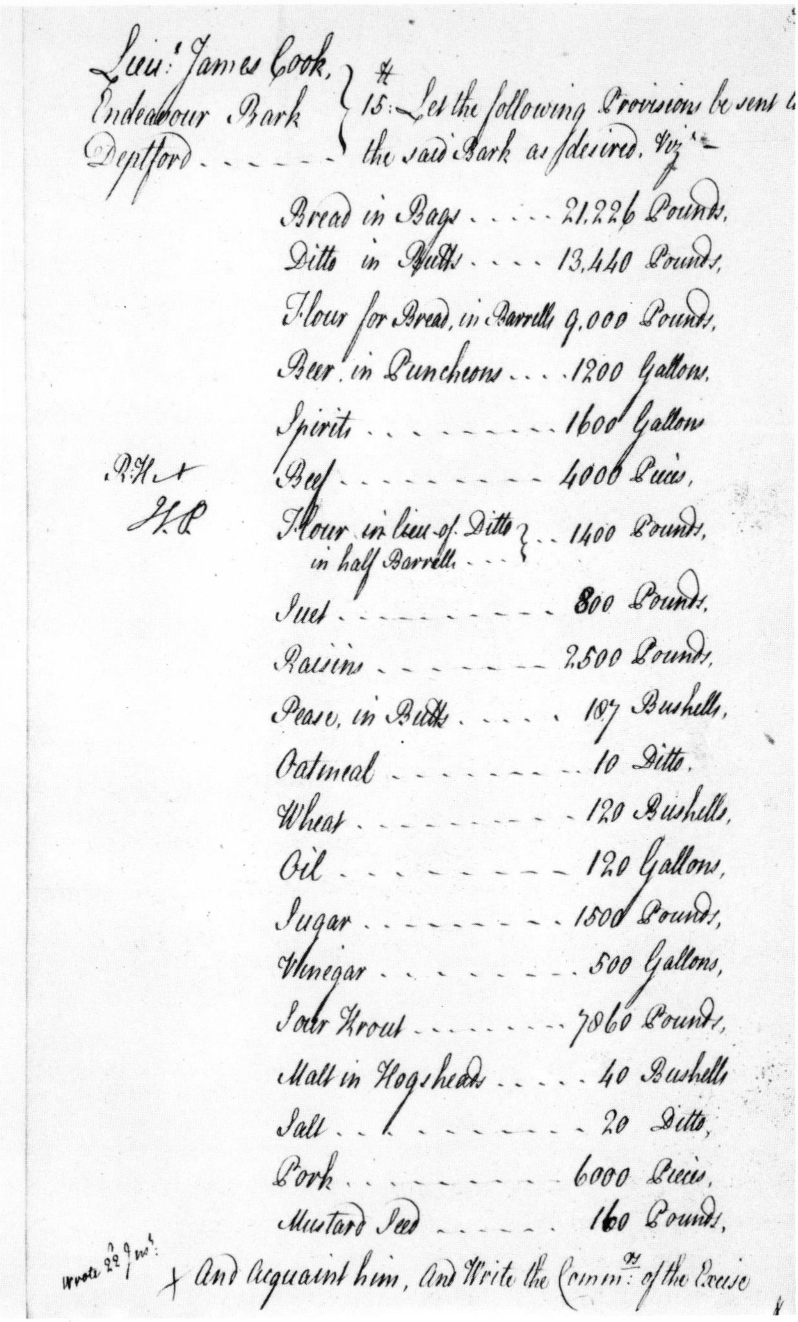

Lieu: James Cook,
Endeavour Bark
Deptford ————

15: Let the following Provisions be sent to
the said Bark as desired. Viz:—

Bread in Bags . . . . . 21,226 Pounds,
Ditto in Butts . . . . 13,440 Pounds,
Flour for Bread, in Barrells 9,000 Pounds,
Beer in Puncheons . . . 1200 Gallons,
Spirits . . . . 1600 Gallons
Beef . . . . 4000 Pieces,
Flour in lieu of Ditto
in half Barrells . . . . 1400 Pounds,
Suet . . . . 800 Pounds,
Raisins . . . . 2,500 Pounds,
Pease, in Butts . . . . . 187 Bushells,
Oatmeal . . . . 10 Ditto,
Wheat . . . . 120 Bushells,
Oil . . . . 120 Gallons,
Sugar . . . . 1500 Pounds,
Vinegar . . . . 500 Gallons,
Sour Krout . . . . 7860 Pounds,
Malt in Hogsheads . . . . 40 Bushells
Salt . . . . 20 Ditto,
Pork . . . . 6000 Pieces,
Mustard Seed . . . . . . 160 Pounds,

And Acquaint him, And Write the Commrs of the Excise

A victualling list from the *Endeavour* period. Note the substantial
entry for 'Sour Krout', a vegetable essential to Cook's constant
campaign against scurvy

rapidly and incurably addicted – and preserved sauerkraut which Cook was to use so successfully in his fight against that medical scourge of the tropics – scurvy.)

Then they had to have a complete carpenter's shop and a complete blacksmith's shop. They had to carry vast reserves of sails and ropes, for both could be expected to wear out several times over in a voyage of this duration. They had to have arms and ammunition, ammunition not only for the hand-guns but also for the twelve swivel guns that the *Endeavour* carried. They had to carry considerable stocks of goods for trading with the wide variety of natives they expected to meet, they had to have a complete range of medical equipment – the *Endeavour* carried a full-time surgeon – and in addition they carried with them a very large store of scientific impedimenta which was essential for making an accurate observation of the transit of Venus. There were no wide open spaces aboard the *Endeavour*.

The complement of the *Endeavour* formed as motley a collection as the cargo they had to take along with them. As his second in command, Cook had Zachary Hicks, many years his junior but an accomplished seaman. His second officer, John Gore, had already been round the world with Wallis, who had but recently returned to England. There were about forty able seamen, a handful of midshipmen, twelve marines, clerks, servants – eight of them – and the scientific party appointed by the Royal Society.

The most important of this last group was Joseph Banks, a member of the Royal Society and an immensely wealthy young man who, instead of devoting his time, as was the custom those days, to the better-class clubs in London, had elected to become a natural scientist and was already an extremely gifted and enthusiastic botanist. There was no question but that Banks had bought his way aboard the *Endeavour* – he was reported to have paid £10,000 – a fortune in those days – for the privilege, but Banks wasn't along just for the fun of it. His dedication to his chosen way of life was complete as he later showed when he became President of the Royal Society, a post he held for almost half a century, during which time he was the undisputed ruler of the scientific world in Britain.

Along with him Banks brought a Dr Carl Solander, a Swede and a famous botanist; Alexander Buchan, a landscape artist, and Sydney Parkinson, an artist who was to make pictorial recordings of all the fauna they caught; Sporing, who was loosely defined as a scientific secretary; and four servants, two of whom were negroes. Independently of them came the Royal Society's official astronomer, Charles Green, who was to share with Cook the responsibility for the actual observation of the transit. The complement was fully made up by a goat, but this was no ordinary goat – it had already circumnavigated the world with Wallis. It's purpose – to supply the officers with fresh milk.

But even in this, the most lavishly equipped and best-manned expedition ever to leave England, some little thing had to go wrong, and did. The man appointed to the position of senior cook turned out to have only one leg, a considerable drawback for a man at sea. Understandably annoyed, Cook demanded that he be replaced at once. He was – by a man with one hand.

By this time both the Admiralty and the Royal Society had studied the implications of the recently returned Wallis's report and the Society requested of the Admiralty that the Venus transit be observed from Tahiti, a request with which the Admiralty readily agreed, partly, it may be, because Tahiti was one of the few islands in the Pacific the latitude and longitude of which were known with any degree of precision but chiefly, one suspects, because the Admiralty didn't care where Cook went in the Pacific as long as he turned south in search of the alleged southern continent as soon as the transit had been observed and recorded.

A two-foot focus Gregorian reflecting telescope made for Cook's transit of Venus observations

The *Endeavour* sailed from Plymouth in August, 1768. The journey south to Madeira, reached on 13 September, was quite uneventful, but the moment of arrival was sadly marred: as they were dropping anchor the master's mate became entangled with the rope, was carried down to the bottom of the harbour and found to be dead when the rope was hauled up again. It is significant and characteristic of the times that his death did not appear to have had any markedly depressing effect on the crew. That is not to say that life was cheap in those days, it was just that death was received with a stoical acceptance of a degree unknown in our Western cultures of today. Especially for seamen voyaging to the tropics, death was an almost inevitable and inseparable part of life. A ship's captain who made a round journey to the Pacific counted himself fortunate if he came back with seventy-five percent of his original crew still alive.

In Madeira they took aboard considerable stores of water and wine – when one takes into account the amount of rum and wine consumed by each person daily in the Navy at that time, one marvels that the *Endeavour* got as far as the Isle of Wight, far less round the world – fresh beef, fresh fruit, vegetables and onions. All of those Cook assumed – and rightly – to be of major importance in the fighting of scurvy, and he insisted that his crew eat them all, in addition to the regular standby of sauerkraut. The first case of Cook administering punishment on the voyage occurred when he found two of his crew breaking his dietary regulations, in this case refusing to eat fresh meat. He had them both flogged. This may seem a severe punishment for so slight an offence, but Cook, as his crews' health records over the next few years were to show, had every justification for his strictness: no ships of that era were ever so little bedevilled by scurvy as the ones Cook commanded.

They crossed the equator, heading for the coast of South America. There was enough and more to keep Banks and his scientific colleagues busy. By the use of nets and guns and fishing lines they were able to catch large numbers of aquatic and aerial forms of life which were all duly brought to the Great Cabin right aft on the poop: there the scientists would spend hours every day dissecting, preserving, classifying and drawing their specimens: when the time came that *Endeavour* was able to make landfalls the botanists brought back so many unknown species of flora that the activity in the Great Cabin would continue from the earliest light of dawn till dusk fell.

A drawing by Sydney Parkinson (the botanist and draughtsman who accompanied Banks on the first voyage) of the blue-black grassquit (*Volatinia jacarina*), a Brazilian bird

As the *Endeavour* sailed down the South American coast, Cook decided to call in at the then Portuguese settlement of Rio de Janeiro for fresh water and supplies of fresh food – it would be their last opportunity to stock up for many thousands of miles. 'From the reception former ships have met with here,' Cook wrote, 'I doubt not but that we should be well received.'

His confidence was sadly misplaced. He sent his First Lieutenant ashore in the pinnace and as soon as Hicks set foot on land he was promptly arrested. An armed guard put out from the shore and officers came aboard and questioned Cook very closely on the reason for his visit there. It became quickly very clear that neither his interrogators nor their Viceroy ashore believed for one moment that the *Endeavour* was a Royal Naval vessel. One finds it difficult to blame them for it would be impossible to conceive of anything less like a man-o'-war than that hulking North Sea coal-boat. They had to be buccaneers or smugglers or illicit traders or just plain spies. They regarded Cook's King's Commission as a forgery and were not at all amused by Cook's explanation about the observation of the transit of Venus owing to the fact that they knew there was no such thing.

Eventually Cook managed to get Hicks released and received permission to bring water and fresh stores aboard, an activity that was carried out in an atmosphere that ranged between armed neutrality and watchful hostility. No member of the crew, except Cook himself, was allowed ashore, although Banks and his two servants managed to make illicit visits there and collect several hundred botanical specimens.

The unfriendly reception received in Rio coupled with the fact that adverse head winds delayed their departure meant

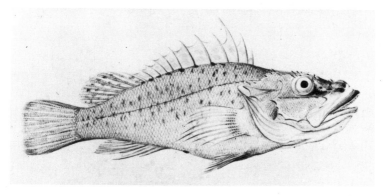

A scorpion fish (*Pontinus kuhlii*) drawn by Sydney Parkinson on the same voyage and observed off Madeira

that the intended brief visit to that port cost Captain Cook no less than twenty-four days. It is interesting to note that this normally placid – one might almost say abnormally placid – man was as capable of fury as the next man: his letters to the Admiralty reporting those events leave no room for doubt.

They sailed on 7 December. Christmas Day was spent in an area about half way between Rio and Cape Horn and from notes made by both Cook and Banks the following day it would appear that the *Endeavour's* crew did not allow the great distance that separated them from their homes and loved ones to interfere with the traditional yuletide spirit. 'Christmas Day,' Banks reports. 'All good Christians, that is to say all hands, got abominably drunk so that at night there was scarce a sober man on the ship: wind, thank God, very moderate or the lord knows what would have become of us.' Cook contented himself with merely noting: 'Yesterday being Christmas Day the people were none of the soberest.' As the normal daily liquid – or liquor – ration of each crew member consisted of as much small beer as he could drink and either a pint of wine or half-pint of rum or brandy one can only contemplate with awe the scenes that must have taken place aboard the *Endeavour* that Christmas Day in 1768.

This was another and almost atypical aspect of Cook's character. He could, on occasion, be a very tolerant man. He was a firm disciplinarian, but not a harsh one – even although he wasn't above, on occasion, having a delinquent's ears cut off for some particularly heinous offence. But when the occasion warranted it and there was no pressing danger or need for alertness, Cook was perfectly prepared to let the crew relax – in the only method they knew how – while he turned a blind eye and deaf ear to the proceedings. On one occasion indeed, they relaxed to such an extent that Cook felt constrained to put them ashore and wait patiently for two days until they were fit to resume their duties.

To the public of his time and to generations thereafter

Cook seemed a stern, remote, withdrawn man. To his officers and men he was a father-figure that they revered to just this side of idolatry. Five years later when Cook was gravely ill with a gall-bladder infection, members of the crew – of the *Resolution*, in this case – spoke of the atmosphere of loss and desolation that hung over the ship. When he finally did reappear on deck, pale and shaken, one diarist noted that you could see the delight in everybody's face from the highest officer to the meanest boy aboard the ship: and it is worth observing that this was the opinion of a certain notorious marine whom Cook had regularly and repeatedly had flogged for drunkenness on duty and attempted desertions at various islands in the Pacific. Wrote the surgeon's mate on the *Resolution* after Cook's death: 'In every situation he stood unrivalled and alone: on him all eyes were turned: he was our leading-star, which at its setting left us involved in darkness and despair.'

As they approached Cape Horn the weather steadily deteriorated just as the temperature steadily dropped until the crew, huddled in their Fearnought jackets, were forced to take all refuge possible from the icy gales that threw the little *Endeavour* about as though she were a piece of drifting flotsam. Too little has been made of the sheer physical hardship that those men had to endure in ships like those in times like those. The watches were long, the work arduous. Living quarters were incredibly cramped and the staple diet of salt pork and weevily biscuits or bread beggar description. But by far the worst factor of all was the state of almost continuous near-exhaustion. Those sailing craft were seldom if ever still. They pitched and they rolled and they yawed and laboured and corkscrewed and every waking minute those cold and tired and hungry men had to brace themselves against the incessant motion of the vessel: any person who has ever spent as much as a couple of hours aboard a ship in bad weather will know how quickly the reserves of physical energy can be drained in

43

such conditions. Sometimes the crew of the *Endeavour* had to put up with gales for weeks on end; sometimes they were at sea for months on end: invariably, when they arrived at the end of a voyage or the end of a leg of a voyage, they did so in a state of complete exhaustion. On one occasion, on arriving at Cape Town after a particularly appalling voyage, the crew staggered ashore – anything to get their feet on the solid earth again – then dropped down and slept by the roadside. It is little wonder that whenever they made a landfall at the end of a long voyage Captain Cook would permit his men to relax in their customary fashion and give them a few days to recover a measure of both health and strength.

It is to be noted that the icy conditions the *Endeavour* was now experiencing as they approached Cape Horn occurred during the middle of January – the period of high summer in the southern hemisphere. It is further to be noted that, years later, Cook was to sail more than another unbelievable thousand miles nearer the South Pole.

On 12 January 1769, the *Endeavour* was standing off the incredibly bleak desolation that is Tierra del Fuego, the island at the very south of the American continent. At Banks' request – so that he, Banks, and his scientific colleagues could go ashore and gather botanical specimens – Cook put into an inlet that he called the Bay of Good Success. Parenthetically, he was the place-namer *par excellence*. He unquestionably gave more names to more places than any other person who has ever lived. Bays, inlets, rivers, promontories, capes, mountains, islands – Cook had only to clap eyes on it and it was as good as named. It does seem rather unfortunate that in doing so he saw fit to exhaust almost the entire nomenclature of the British aristocracy – Cook never mentioned his political leanings and he certainly didn't have to either – the Lords of the Admiralty and divers influential patrons of his own, but, then, one supposes he had to get his names from somewhere. With very few exceptions, as, for instance, when a few

Natives of Tierra del Fuego whose huts, Cook wrote in his *Journal*, 'are made like a beehive' and who 'must be a very hardy race' as the huts are 'neither proof against wind, hail, rain, or snow'

Pacific islands reverted to their original native names, nearly all the names Cook gave have remained. It is tragically ironic that the name he gave to one of his most important discoveries, a group of islands in the North Pacific, did not remain but reverted to the original. Cook called them the Sandwich Isles, after his friend and patron Lord Sandwich. They are now known by their original name of Hawaii: it was on the beaches of Hawaii that Cook was to meet his death.

Banks and his party went ashore and returned before evening in a high state of excitement, bearing with them scores of botanical specimens quite unknown in Europe. Two days later Banks led a party of a dozen people ashore, their destination some low peaks a few miles inland. However, the going was slow – they encountered an unexpected swamp – and they had not yet reached the mountains when the sky became overcast and it began to snow. Then Alexander Buchan, the landscape artist, had an epileptic fit – he was known to be an epileptic and why he was ever allowed aboard the *Endeavour* in the first place must remain forever a mystery. They made him comfortable and lit a fire to keep him warm. Banks and three others pressed on to the hills, had a botanical field-day, and then returned to where they had left the rest of the party. Buchan was much recovered so Banks decided to return to the ship immediately.

Unfortunately, the snow now began to fall very heavily indeed, slowing up progress, and it was next morning before they arrived back aboard. During the course of the night both of Banks' negro servants died, an occurrence due not so much to their inability to withstand cold as to the fact that, during Banks' absence in the hills, they had disposed of the expedition's rum supply.

The *Endeavour* continued on her way through Le Maire Strait and round Cape Horn. There was none of the battling against mountainous seas usually associated with the rounding of this cape. The weather had improved dramatically, the sun shone, the seas were calm, so Cook, typically and knowing he had time in hand, made his way round at a very leisurely pace, sounding, surveying, charting, and taking very accurate fixes of latitude and longitude.

The day of the rounding of Cape Horn was unquestionably a momentous event, a watershed in the history of the Pacific Ocean. It changed the course of Pacific history. Whether that change was to be for good or ill – most people would say ill and I would whole-heartedly agree with them – is not here relevant to the story of Cook's voyages, except in so far that Cook himself often expressed the fear that where the white man went, the white man being epitomised by himself in the Pacific, degradation, despoliation and disaster would, whether soon or late, inevitably follow. What is certain is that from 24 January 1769, the Pacific was never to be the same again.

Other people had been in those waters before Cook, of course. Drake had been and Quiros, but their passing had left no mark. The gallant and dashing Bougainville, the French sailor-adventurer who had slipped through the British blockade of the St. Lawrence at the very time when Cook had been there, had visited Tahiti briefly and then gone on his way. Tasman, too, had touched upon those waters but that had

Sydney Parkinson's drawing of the red-tailed tropic bird (*Phaeton rubricanda*)

been at the Western or Australian (then New Holland) end. Commodore Byron, Foul Weather Jack, had sailed clear across the Pacific without seeing a soul or a soul seeing him, so he hardly counted. And Wallis had been in Tahiti, but that was the only place where he had been.

Now, for the first time, there moved into the Pacific a man who could find his way precisely and accurately to wherever he wanted to go, a man who, when he left a place, would always know exactly where he had been. Here was a man destined to scour the Pacific, to make enormously far-reaching sweeps on a scale undreamed of by any previous explorer, to discover more islands and leave the imprint of the white man on more peoples than all his predecessors put together. Here was the man, the cynics would say, who was going to open up the Pacific to the benefits and riches of modern Western civilization. Whole books have, in fact, been written roundly condemning Cook for the ever-lasting damage he was responsible for wreaking on the Pacific. Alas, merely because a man can write a book it doesn't mean that he can't be silly, and such writers are very silly indeed. If it hadn't been Cook, it would have been someone else. Could anyone possibly be so naive as to imagine that if Cook had never lived that the Pacific would still be a trackless and undiscovered waste? It so happened that when it was ripe for the man, the hour and the place to come together, blind Destiny reached out and tapped Cook on the shoulder.

The *Endeavour* sailed serenely north-westwards under fine conditions, a pleasant if slightly monotonous trip marred only by the disappearance of a young marine over the side. It was said that he had been caught stealing a piece of sealskin to make a purse and rather than face Cook had chosen to commit suicide. It does seem a highly unlikely tale.

On 13 April 1769, eight months after leaving England, the *Endeavour* arrived in Tahiti. They arrived, astonishingly, without one man on the sick-list, without one case of scurvy,

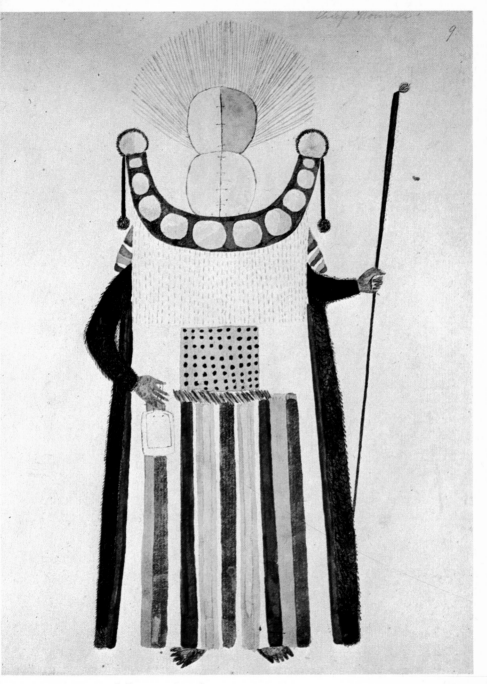

A Tahitian in full mourning dress

The Bay of Good Success, Tierra del Fuego. The artist,
Alexander Buchan, died in Tahiti later in the voyage

A Maori and one of the *Endeavour*'s crew exchanging a
handkerchief for a crayfish. Painted by an unidentified
crew member

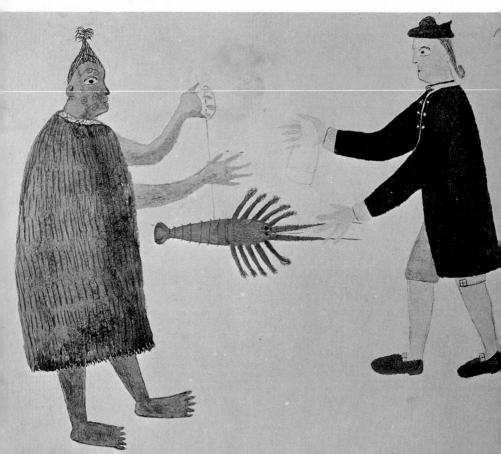

which after eight months at sea in those days was a feat just within the bounds of credibility. It was a splendid tribute to Cook's insistence on adhering to dietary regulations. Sauerkraut was unquestionably the first line of defence against the disease. In the beginning – Cook himself relates this in his journal – he had the greatest difficulty in making his men eat this outlandish foreign dish but he solved this problem by having his officers eat it with such tremendous gusto and to the accompaniment of such loudly admiring remarks that curiosity led some of the crew to sample it, which they did in ever-increasing amounts and numbers until eventually Cook was compelled to ration it. One is slightly puzzled as to why he did not try some such form of psychology and guileful persuasion with the two men whom he had had flogged in Madeira for refusing to eat fresh meat: presumably some practical problems arose when it came to the question of flogging the entire crew.

CHAPTER 3

CHARTING
NEW ZEALAND

IT is customary, if not obligatory, I have observed, for the biographers of Captain Cook who have accompanied him as far as his first landfall of Tahiti to halt there awhile then sit back and rest for about twenty pages while they go on rhapsodising about the beauties and wonders of this sun-drenched tropical paradise, about the blue skies and bluer

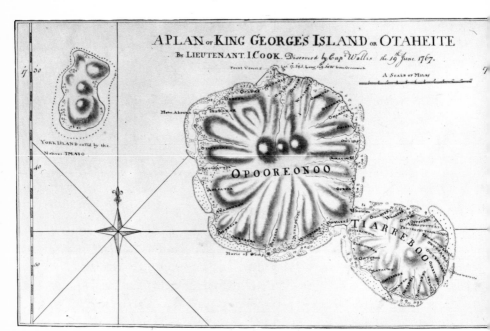

Cook's plan of Tahiti showing Point Venus and Matavai Bay on the northernmost tip. Tahiti was discovered by Captain Wallis on 19 June 1767

seas, about the white torrents gushing from forest-clad mountain slopes, about the nodding palms and golden sands (actually, they were black where Cook landed in Matavai Bay). It is certainly *de rigeur* to dwell at sentimental length on the golden people who inhabited this other Eden, the handsome men, the gorgeous girls, their simple natural form of life, their affectionate natures and, in short, the wholly Utopian nature of their existence.

Now, apart from noting in the passing that those self-same golden boys and girls were much given to infanticide, ritual murder, the waging of the most bloodily ferocious internecine tribal warfare in Polynesia and indulging in the practice of theft and pickpocketing on a scale and with an expertise that would have made Fagin turn in his union card – apart from that, I say, there is little to be said against this approach. Still trying to preserve this fairness of approach, it must be admitted that there is nothing to be said for it either. It's pleasant, but it's irrelevant. For a straight historical narrative a briefly sketched in background suffices: a Rembrandt or a Turner is not called for – and, besides, the travelogue books do it a whole lot better. Moreover, everyone has his own image of Tahiti, the most romantically famous island in the world: if he hasn't heard of it then he's obviously illiterate and wouldn't be reading this book anyway. Let us, then, take Tahiti for read.

As soon as the *Endeavour* anchored in Matavai Bay literally hundreds of canoes came out from shore and surrounded her. The natives were gay and friendly and cheerful and colourful: Cook treated them with caution. His second officer, Gore, who had sailed with Wallis in the *Dolphin* and had been there two years previously had warned him about the volatility and occasional treachery of the Polynesian people. When two of the *Dolphin's* boats had first landed they had been attacked by spears and stones and Wallis had been forced to fire at his attackers, killing one and wounding

Captain Wallis defending himself during his Tahitian landing

others. Even after that the *Dolphin* had been opposed by a force of hundreds of canoes and thousands of men and had to achieve a landing by force, backed by their guns, before the Tahitians would accept defeat.

But the happy throng that had come out to meet them on this occasion bore no resemblance to a war party. A former local chief O'whaha – the spelling is as good as any, the variations of spelling of any one name tend to be legion – spotted Gore and welcomed him warmly. From then on their welcome was assured.

The first two days were spent in getting to know that particular section of the island and the people who mattered on it, in establishing bartering norms for fresh food supplies and in learning to keep their hands in their pockets which was the only way they could prevent the contents from disappearing.

Cook decided to set up his Venus transit observatory on shore: apart from giving him a completely stable platform from which to make his observations it would also give him a great deal more elbow room than he could hope to obtain on the crowded deck of the *Endeavour*. For a site for his observatory – it was to be known as the fort – Cook picked a sandy spit at the north-east end of Matavai Bay. This situation had the double advantage of being closely covered by the *Endeavour's* guns should any trouble arise, while, close by, the river, the Vaipupu, which debouched into the sea just on the other side of the spit, would provide them with all the fresh water they required.

On 15 April, two days after their arrival, Cook took a party ashore to the fort site. Here he marked out the perimeter of the site and the building began. It was a pretty primitive affair, consisting of earthworks on three sides with deep ditches beyond, the earthworks being topped by palisades cut from the nearby woods: on the east, facing the river, they used ship's casks. A gateway was constructed and then

Cook's own drawing of Fort Venus on Tahiti

tents pitched inside the fortification walls, on which were now mounted guns brought from the ship. The tents were for the use of the crew, the scientists, the officers, the observatory, for the blacksmith's equipment and for the kitchen. The most willing helpers of all in the construction were the Tahitians themselves who apparently failed to realise that the fort was being constructed primarily as a defence against themselves.

Beyond and surrounding the fort a line was made: this, the Tahitians were told, they were not at any time to cross. Unfortunately, the Tahitians were not very good at doing what they were told and this, coupled with their inborn propensity for theft, led to the death of one of them. One day, when Banks and Cook were out duck shooting they heard the sound of a shot coming from the fort. They ran back and found a Tahitian lying dead on the ground: of the large numbers of other natives who had been gathered around the fort only a short time previously there was now no sign.

As almost invariably happens on the occasion of sudden and violent action witnesses disagreed freely with each other as to how things had happened. *What* had happened was beyond dispute: a native had pushed an unsuspecting sentry, snatched his musket, ran away with it and had been shot down.

Understandably, it was quite some time before the men of the *Endeavour* and the Tahitians were on speaking terms again. Cook, through O'whaha, explained just how grave an offence it was to steal a musket and the Tahitians agreed that if a person felt that an offence had been committed against him then he was perfectly at liberty to take whatsoever action he chose to retaliate. This was their own code. Cook appears to have been satisfied that they had taken his point, learnt their lesson and now understood how bad a thing theft was. Almost certainly, they understood nothing of the kind and probably privately wondered what all the fuss was about. The Tahitians weren't, it seems clear, an immoral people; they were just happily amoral. Almost certainly they didn't understand the meaning of the word 'theft'. For them, if you saw a thing and wanted it you just took it. It was as simple as that. From their point of view if there were any lessons to be learnt from Cook's stern admonitions it was that they should be more careful the next time they set about acquiring the white man's property. The thievery, it need hardly be added, continued unabated.

In spite of this, relations between the English and the Tahitians were excellent. Even making allowances for nostalgia's golden glow, it does appear to have been a blissful, an almost idyllic period. Letters and journal made it clear that there was in the Tahiti of that time an extraordinarily Arcadian atmosphere that they had never encountered before and were never to encounter again. It is impossible for us today to recapture the spirit and the mood of the time for a Gauguin's 'Nevermore', that infinitely

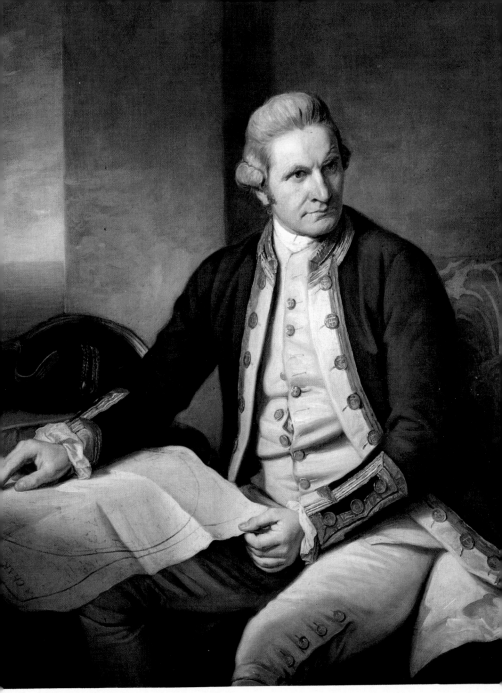

A portrait by Nathaniel Dance painted in 1776, the year in which Cook set off on his last journey

Stone monuments on Easter Island painted by William Hodges

The *Adventure* (foreground) and *Resolution* in the Antarctic.
The *Adventure* is taking on ice to melt for drinking water

sad picture of an unsmiling Tahitian girl, shows, it is gone forever.

But it certainly wasn't gone then. A remarkable amount of socialising and fraternisation took place. Cook and his officers, dining almost nightly with local chiefs, either in their homes or aboard ship, took care of the socialising side, while his crew, with the willing help of the cheerfully accommodating Tahitian girls, took care of the fraternisation. 'They struck up friendships' one acid observer sniffed, 'that were not of a platonic nature.' But that, in the second half of the eighteenth century, was an exceptional attitude: tolerance was the order of the day, and no one showed more than Cook: not only did he know what was going on – when he saw the Tahitian girls boarding his ship at nightfall he'd have been pretty obtuse not to – he didn't even bother to turn a blind eye to it. It has to be remembered that the dead hand of repressive Victorian morality lay almost a hundred years in the future.

The honeymoon came to an abrupt end on 2 May. On that day the astronomical instruments were taken ashore and transported to the fort, where they were placed in the observatory tent under an armed guard. Chief among those instruments was the quadrant, which was absolutely essential for observing the transit of Venus. This was a very heavy instrument encased in a wooden box.

When Cook was making his customarily thorough rounds that day he found tent, guard and box all where they should have been: the quadrant, however, had vanished. It is not too difficult to imagine the consternation and fury of Cook and the scientists: without this instrument, as far as the transit was concerned, the *Endeavour* might as well have stayed in England.

Cook at once ordered the bay sealed off so that the culprit could not escape by sea. He was about to interrogate the local chiefs when one of them, Tuborai, more intelligent

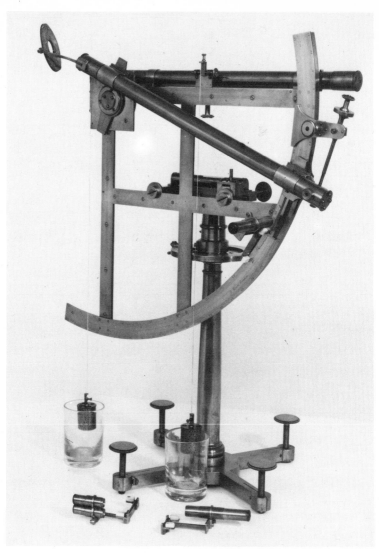

A quadrant made in 1768 and one such as Cook used

than the rest or at least sufficiently intelligent to realise that this was going to be an extraordinarily unhappy day for Tahiti if Captain Cook didn't get his quadrant back immediately, took Banks aside and said he knew the identity of the thief – who had prudently taken to the hills.

Banks, accompanied by Green – after all, he was the astronomer and it was *his* quadrant – and a midshipman, took off in pursuit. Tuborai went with them as guide, enquiring from house to house as to the direction the thief had taken, information which was cheerfully and willingly given. They walked and ran for a distance of almost seven miles – mostly uphill, as Banks said bitterly, and in a temperature of 91° in the shade – before they met a group of people, but not understandably the thief himself, carrying a somewhat battered quadrant, or, more precisely, a part of it. The other missing parts soon came in – the Tahitians had belatedly, but not too late, realised that this time they had gone too far. The damaged quadrant, it was found, could be repaired. After the customary cooling-off period of twenty four hours to allow anger to evaporate on the one side and sulks on the other, the honeymoon was resumed.

The third of June came, the skies remained satisfactorily clear and the transit of Venus was successfully observed from two points on the island and a third on the neighbouring island of Moorea. Cook and Green were certain that they had achieved excellent results. In point of fact, they hadn't. It was no fault of theirs – no observers anywhere in the world achieved the results they had hoped for: instruments for astronomical observation had not at that time been refined to a sufficiently high degree.

Almost another six weeks were to elapse before the *Endeavour* left Tahiti. True, Cook circumnavigated the island, charting it in his usual highly accurate fashion: the hull of the vessel had to be cleaned, the long-boat repaired and the fort dismantled, but that should not have taken more than a week. Restowing all the gear that had been taken to the fort and provisioning the ship for the long voyage ahead should not have taken more than another. Although, very understandably, no mention of this is made in any report or log, the reason for the delay seems very clear: from Cook downwards, the men of the *Endeavour* just could not bring themselves to leave the golden lotus-land that was Tahiti, and sought to delay their departure by whatever legitimate means was possible.

Just before they left a significant event occurred that merits recording because of its future implications. Two marines, Webb and Gibson, deserted and took to the hills with their girl friends and had a message transmitted to Cook to the effect that they had no intention of returning. Cook regarded this as a very grave matter indeed. It was a serious challenge to discipline, an undermining of his personal authority. He needed every single man he had aboard the ship. And, if they were permitted to get off with it, a considerable number of others might emulate them for few people aboard the *Endeavour* would have found it any great hardship to settle down permanently in Tahiti.

Cook reacted with typical speed and energy. He seized half a dozen local chiefs and held them hostage. As well they might be, the chiefs were bitterly resentful of this treatment: they had been in no way responsible for the voluntary disappearance of the two marines. Cook didn't even argue with them, just stated flatly that they would be released when the two marines were returned to the ship, and as Cook had a remarkable ability of convincing people that he meant every word he said, immediate action was forthcoming. Native guides led a ship's party into the hills and Webb and Gibson were returned in very short order indeed.

This incident is significant because it represents the first instance of a technique that Cook was to employ again and again in the Pacific. Whenever anything of importance was stolen or any serious crime committed, Cook promptly seized local chiefs and held them as hostages until either the stolen object was returned or the malefactor handed over.

As a technique it was as effective as it was brilliantly simple and it worked like a charm time and time again – until the last time. Then it didn't work and Cook was to die because of it.

The sailing of the *Endeavour* was a heart-rending affair. The English and the Tahitians had become extremely fond of each other and there was heart-break on both sides. Many of the men were leaving behind Tahitian girls with whom, given the choice, they would have settled down permanently. Even on the day of departure, the chiefs who had come aboard the *Endeavour* to say goodbye implored them not to go, tears streaming down their faces. And when the *Endeavour* finally raised anchor and moved slowly away the bay was filled with hundreds of canoes each with its complement of bitterly lamenting men and women. By any standards it must have been a very moving spectacle.

When Cook sailed he took with him a local chief by the name of Tupia – this was at Tupia's insistent request – and his boy servant, Tiata. Tupia was not a native Tahitian but came from the island of Raiatea to the west. There were many other islands there, he said, and he knew them well. He had relatives on some of the islands which he had occasionally visited socially: even more islands he had visited on a less social basis as a member of war canoe expeditions. He would, Cook realised, be a very useful man indeed to have around, both as a guide and a translator.

Cook sailed first of all to the island of Huahine, where he was well received, then to Raiatea: local legend had it that New Zealand had been colonised from that island. Cook visited and charted several more islands in this group and gave them the name Society Islands – 'Because of their contiguity'. He did not, of course, forget to annex them in the name of the British crown.

Cook's secret orders from the Admiralty had been to

A double canoe off Raiatea, Society Islands

penetrate as far south as latitude 40° in search of the Southern Continent. Cook himself generally held a pretty open mind on speculative matters – his attitude appears to have been that it was not his job to hold opinions but to find out the answers to questions – but in this instance he appears to have been doubtful from the beginning as to the existence of this fabled continent, a doubt that had been very strongly reinforced since he had met Tupia who had a really phenomenal knowledge of the south central Pacific but who was not, he said, the traveller that his father had been. His father, he said, had travelled a great way to the south and there was no land there, only islands. But, to Cook, orders were orders. He headed the *Endeavour* south.

He took her south for close on 1,500 miles until he had

reached the latitude of 40° south, the prescribed limit imposed by the Admiralty, without finding any sign of land. Already, Alexander Dalrymple's theory had been badly dented. Cook was not disposed to hang around. The weather was abominable, whole gales were the order of the day, constant repairs had to be carried out to the sails and the rigging, and the crew was reaching a state of exhaustion. In short, the Roaring Forties were living up to their name. Cook turned to the north-west in search of better conditions, found them, turned to the west and then fixed on a course that was roughly W.S.W. On this course they continued for about three weeks, during which time nothing untoward happened except for the demise of a boatswain's mate who had mistakenly assumed that he could cope with a full bottle of Navy rum. Altogether, now, six members of the original complement had been lost. (Early in the stay in Tahiti Alexander Buchan, the landscapist, had had a fatal attack of epilepsy.)

On 7 October a youngster by the name of Nicholas Young sighted land from the mast-head. The boy was known throughout the ship as Young Nick so Cook immediately named the promontory Young Nick's Head, a fitting enough honour for Young Nick's were the first European eyes ever to see the East Coast of New Zealand.

Cook knew it was New Zealand. New Zealand was known to exist but that was just about all that was known about it. Tasman, the only other Pacific explorer who came anywhere near Cook's stature as a navigator and seaman, had visited the west coast of New Zealand 126 years previously in the course of an epic voyage which had started from Batavia in the Dutch East Indies and which apart from the discovery of Tasmania, which Tasman assumed to be joined to Australia (so did Cook for that matter – he never checked to see if it was an island; he had no reason to), and New Zealand, also included the circumnavigation of Australia: Tasman, for some reason, took a very wide sweep out through

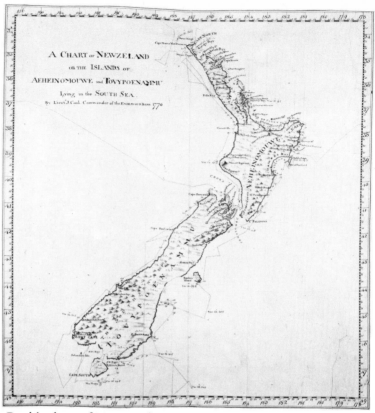

Cook's chart of New Zealand

the Pacific and never went near the east coast of Australia.

New Zealand, then, had been discovered, but that was just about all. Nobody had seen it since Tasman's time. And Tasman had left little enough information about it. He had sailed the length of the west coast of North Island and some distance down the west coast of South Island. He never tried to find his way round to the east coast. He didn't sail far enough south to find out whether New Zealand was an island or whether it was joined to some great land mass further to the south. He did not, strangely enough, investigate the passage between North and South Island, now known

64

as Cook Strait, although there are definite indications in his journal that he suspected that such a strait might exist. Or maybe he was just in a hurry to get to the Fiji Isles which was to be his next port of call. Tasman, though a great sailor, lacked Cook's iron will and determination to investigate everything to the bitter end. Tasman's superiors in Batavia were aware of this and reproached him for leaving everything 'to be examined by more industrious successors'.

Cook was to be that industrious successor. Along with some of his men, the first Europeans ever to set foot on New Zealand (in the previous century the Maoris had been so unremittingly hostile that Tasman had prudently never attempted a landing) he landed on the east bank of the river Waipoua, the site of the modern Gisborne, which is about half-way up the east coast of North Island.

Seldom, if ever, can the discovery of a new land have been attended by more inauspicious circumstances. There were Maoris on the far bank and they were clearly hostile. (One finds it difficult to blame them, even if they were hostile for the wrong reason: the colossal arrogance of the western European nations who roamed the world annexing everything in sight, regardless of the thoughts or wishes of the rightful owners of those regions, is quite stupefying.) Cook and some men crossed the river in their yawl – the pinnace remaining behind – to try to establish some sort of contact with the Maoris. Cook and some others disappeared into the trees and no sooner had they done so than a party of Maoris tried to cut off the crew of the yawl. The men in the pinnace fired warning shots over the Maoris' heads, but still they advanced upon the yawl. The next shot from the pinnace was not a warning shot: a Maori was killed instantly. Cook and his men retired to the *Endeavour*. End of round one.

The following morning Cook and a party went ashore again and approached a group of heavily armed and clearly truculent natives. Cook and his men offered them presents

Portraits of New Zealand natives by Sydney Parkinson

but they weren't interested in presents, they were interested in the swords that the English were carrying. One tried to wrest Green's sword away, a mêlée broke out and the inevitable happened. The tally this time – one Maori dead, three injured. Cook and his men returned to the *Endeavour*. End of round two.

Cook was not a man to give up easily. In the afternoon he had himself rowed around the bay searching for a spot where he might land unopposed. Everywhere, however, the surf was too heavy and he had no option than to make his way back to the *Endeavour*. On their way they enountered a couple

Sydney Parkinson's impression of Maoris challenging Cook's men to fight (sticking out the tongue was the customary method of expressing defiance)

of canoes. Tupia addressed them saying that they – the white men – were friends and wished to speak to them. The Maoris started to paddle away as swiftly as they could. Cook ordered a shot to be fired over their heads in the hope that this would make them stop. They stopped all right. They stopped, turned, and came at Cook's boat with all the speed they could muster. They knew enough about musket fire now to associate those bangs with death. Clearly they thought they were going to be killed and if that were the case they might as well die fighting. The tally this time – four Maoris dead.

That was the end of the third round and the end of this hopelessly one-sided contest. Cook, like everyone else aboard the *Endeavour*, was appalled by the happenings of the previous twenty-four hours and realised that to attempt any more landings on this particular stretch of the coast would only precipitate further senseless slaughter. The *Endeavour* weighed anchor and sailed away. Rather sadly or bitterly or both Cook named the place Poverty Bay – 'Because it afforded us no one thing we wanted'. And Poverty Bay it is to this day.

The *Endeavour* moved south round the Mahia Peninsula into Hawke's Bay – Cook named it after the First Lord of the Admiralty – a huge shallow bay about sixty miles across. At the north end of the bay they encountered some Maoris in canoes who were civil and friendly enough but at the southern end they encountered hostile Maoris. One canoe came alongside making a pretence to barter: what they did, in fact, was to try to kidnap young Tiata. Alas for them, like all the other Maoris they came across, they had never heard of the existence of firearms and three of them had to die before the youngster was rescued. Cook promptly called the spot Cape Kidnappers and went on his way.

The further south they went the less likelihood there appeared of finding any harbour. Cook came to the conclusion that there were going to be no suitable harbours for a long way down that coast (he was perfectly right) and decided to go back north. The spot where he retraced his steps he christened, appropriately enough, Cape Turnagain.

It is to be noted that all decisions such as those were Cook's and Cook's alone. His was the entire burden of responsibility and there is no doubt that while his officers were occasionally irritated by his secrecy their trust in him was absolute. It is true that Cook did from time to time carry out a form of democratic consultation with his men but these were usually called merely so that Cook could inform them of decisions he had actually made. But there was one authenticated occasion – this was on his next ship, the *Resolution* – when Cook did ask for general agreement on a proposal. When the allotted time had come for them to return to England he proposed that they should remain for another year in the Pacific and Antarctic! They agreed.

They repassed Hawke's Bay and Poverty Bay and came to a sheltered inlet which provided them with water. The Maoris here were friendly and eager to trade. Through Tupia, who experienced no difficulty at all with the Maori language, they learned that the natives called it Tolaga Bay: for once, Cook let it go at that. Banks and his scientists were in raptures for here they found in the wildest profusion trees, plants, flowers, birds and animals and insects that were quite unknown in any other part of the world.

They continued north, then turned directly almost due west, following the coastline and as they rounded the promontory were threatened by hostile Maoris in huge war canoes. Cook had round shot fired over their heads and they made off for shore at great speed. The promontory, inevitably, became Cape Runaway.

Now they were moving along the shores of a fertile crescent of land which was astonishingly, well cultivated – to such an extent that Cook bestowed on those waters the name of the Bay of Plenty. At the far end of the bay they put into a

This engraving from a drawing by Sydney Parkinson comes from his *Journal of a Voyage to the South Seas*, published in 1784, and it bears the caption: 'The manner in which the New Zealand Warriors defy their enemies'

suitable inlet and here Cook and Green took their astronomical instruments ashore to observe a transit of Mercury. The inlet became, of course, Mercury Bay.

And so they made their way up to the most northerly point of New Zealand with Cook busily naming everything in sight. A look at a large scale map gives the impression that Cook must have been so taken up with this occupation, which clearly delighted him, that he could have had very little time indeed left for charting and navigation.

Cook rested his crew briefly in the Bay of Islands, reputedly the most beautiful in New Zealand, then set off again to the north to attempt the rounding of the northern tip of New Zealand which, from the log entries and navigational fixes Tasman had made the previous century, he knew could not now be very far distant. Nor was it, only about a hundred miles, but Cook was faced with such bad weather and such adverse winds – they blew strongly from the north-west, which was precisely the direction in which Cook wanted to sail – that the lumbering collier, a notoriously poor sailer at the best of times, made practically no progress at all. All the crew suffered horribly and it would have been easy for Cook to take shelter in some convenient inlet and wait for some more propitious moment but then Cook *had* to have something, some very special quality indeed, to make him the greatest explorer in our history. And he had – this diamond-hard determination to achieve a goal he had set himself, an inflexible will that made it impossible for him to abandon a project once embarked upon.

And on Christmas Day, 1769 ('All hands drunk', Banks reports), after two weeks of incessant battling against gale force winds and continuously heavy seas, Cook did indeed achieve his goal. He sighted and identified a group of islands known as the Three Kings, last seen by Tasman a century and a quarter before. Cook knew that he had cleared the north of New Zealand and was now well to the west of its most north-westerly point, Cape Maria van Diemen, so named by Tasman. Cook turned the *Endeavour* south.

The west coast of North Island was less well charted by Cook than the rest of the country. There were two excellent reasons for this. Firstly, Cook was in a hurry: the *Endeavour* was beginning to leak badly, she had experienced such rough weather ever since leaving Tahiti that the caulking was beginning to come away from the seams; and she was now trailing so much marine growth that it was becoming urgent that it should be removed as soon as possible. For both purposes the *Endeavour* would have to be careened on some suitably sandy beach and that there were none such around on that inhospitable coast Cook was pretty certain. Secondly, they were on a lee shore with the powerful westerlies trying to push the *Endeavour* towards land. 'A very dangerous coast', Cook observed laconically and prudently gave it a very wide berth indeed, with the result that he missed such splendid harbours as Hokianga, Kaipara, Manukau (where the modern city of Auckland now stands) and Kawhia. (Cook was to miss several very important harbours in the following years, including Sydney and Vancouver: this – with the exception of Sydney – was invariably because he was standing far out on a lee shore, or because he sailed past them during the night.)

On the 11 January they raised an 8,000 feet snow-covered mountain cone which Cook called Mount Egmont. Beyond this the coast-line turned to the south-east but instead of following it Cook sailed directly across the mouth of the bight until he reached the northern shores of what we now call South Island, where he turned in an easterly direction, passing Murderers' Bay (now Golden Bay) in memory of members of Tasman's crew who had been slain by the Maoris there while attempting to effect a landing, and Tasman Bay, before arriving at an anchorage that was perfect for his purpose, an inlet almost totally enclosed by hills and provided with a selection of splendid beaches all ideally suited for careening the *Endeavour*. It was the finest harbour Cook had found in all of the South Seas and he was to return here several times in the years to come. He gave it the name of Queen Charlotte Sound.

While his men were scraping and caulking the careened vessel, Cook went climbing. Cook had the extraordinary ability, so uncanny as to be almost clairvoyant, of being able to guess at what lay on the other side of a hill. If he thought there was land close ahead, there would be land ahead. If he thought a coast would tend in a certain direction, it did. If he sighted distant land and thought it would turn out to be an island, an island it would be; if he thought it but part of a much larger land mass, then it would almost certainly be that. There are many instances of disputes between Cook and his officers as to what they were likely to see next or how a newly discovered piece of land would resolve itself: there are no instances of Cook having been wrong. It must have been very exasperating indeed for his officers.

And so Cook went climbing for he was convinced that there must be a strait leading through to the eastern seas. He didn't have to climb very far before he reached an elevation sufficient to show him that his supposition was correct, and on 7 February, with the *Endeavour* ready for sea again, Cook took her through the strait to the east. For once, Banks insisted on naming this passage and as it was one and the same person who had suspected the existence of this passage, had discovered it and was the first to sail through it, Cook Strait seemed a very appropriate choice of name.

Some of the ship's officers still maintained that what they thought was North Island might still be only a peninsula attached to a very much greater land mass to the south-east – Cook had steadily maintained that this was not possible but there is nothing so infuriating as being confronted by a person who is always right so his officers stuck stubbornly to their opinions. Patiently, instead of striking off to the south as he had intended to do immediately, Cook turned the *Endeavour* to the north-east and two days later they sighted Cape Turnagain, the starting point for their circumnavigation of the island. This effectively put an end to the argument.

Cook turned south, down past the Cook Strait again (astonishingly, he'd missed what is now Wellington Harbour) then down the east coast of South Island – or what we now know to be South Island. Cook, on the other hand, didn't know whether it was an island or whether it was attached to some southern continental land mass, and, as he didn't want to find out if it were the latter the hard way, he moved very circumspectly down the coast, tacking to and fro in the hours of darkness in waters that they had already established to be safe.

On 17 February, after spending two days running parallel to a range of snow-capped mountains, they sailed by what Cook took to be a large off-shore island which, no doubt as a return compliment for Cook Strait, he named after Banks. This is one of the only two mistakes of any note that Cook made in his circumnavigation of New Zealand. It is in fact a peninsula but the strip of land (on which Christchurch now stands) joining it to the mainland is so low-lying that, from some distance out to sea it is easy to mistake it for an island.

They continued south-west for a few uneventful days along a barren and rather inhospitable coast. As they drew near the south end of the island westerly gales sprang up and drove them well out into the Pacific, and when they turned west again in search of the mainland, having in the mean-time made a good deal of southing, they regained contact not with South Island but with Stewart Island, which is separated from the southernmost point of South Island by the Foveaux Strait, and when they rounded Southwest Cape, Cook was in no doubt at all that they had reached the southern limits of the island for the wide deep ocean swell they now encountered could only have been built up over thousands of miles of ocean. Cook headed the *Endeavour* north, past the magnificent fjords that run deep into the south-west corner of South Island.

Banks and the scientists thought that those fjords would prove very rewarding for botanising and geological research, and heavy pressure was brought to bear on Cook to sail up one of them and anchor. This Cook positively refused to do and for very sound reasons indeed. Those fjords were cliff-sided so that the wind in the fjords could blow in only one of two directions – from the west, up the fjord, or from the

74

(LEFT) Dr Daniel Carl Solander, alleged at the time to be the ablest botanist in England, travelled with Cook in the *Endeavour* on the first voyage

(RIGHT) Sydney Parkinson, from an Edinburgh brewing family, sailed with Cook as a natural history draughtsman on the same voyage as Solander, and like him was a member of Banks's suite

east, down the fjord, and as the prevailing winds were continuously from the west this meant that once the *Endeavour* got inside a fjord she would be unable to get back down again.

A man of Bank's unquestioned intelligence must have appreciated the logic of this, but he still put his angry disappointment on record. Almost certainly the anger was fuelled by an element of chagrin or pique: Banks had tended to go along with Alexander Dalrymple's concept of a southern continent and had firmly believed that the southern part of South Island would be found to be joined to it. But now he saw Cook in the process of demolishing Dalrymple's dream, while at the same time completely disproving his, Banks', own idea. It must have been very vexatious indeed.

For the next two weeks the *Endeavour* sailed north-west up the coast, and a bleak, inhospitable and forbidding coast it was, backed by a range of snow-topped and glaciated mountains – what we now know as the Southern Alps. On 26 March they were back in Queen Charlotte Sound, having completed the circumnavigation of South Island, having in the process completely demolished many myths and misconceptions about the country. The most commonly held idea had been that the land Tasman had discovered was a peninsula jutting out from the great southern continent. Now Cook had proved conclusively that it consisted of two separate islands and that there was no continental land mass anywhere near it. There were going to be a good number of red faces in the Royal Society when Cook returned home with what would be, for them, this bad news.

Apart from mistakenly assuming that Banks Peninsula was an island, Cook's only other error was to regard Stewart Island as a peninsula, and a very understandable error it was, too, because at that point the *Endeavour* had been blown so far to the east and south that when Cook regained contact with land he had no means of knowing that they had passed by the Foveaux Strait in the interval. Those errors apart, Cook's chart of New Zealand is most astonishingly accurate.

CHAPTER 4

AUSTRALIA AND THE GREAT BARRIER REEF

THE *Endeavour* did not remain long in the vicinity of Queen Charlotte Sound. Both the ship and all aboard were in excellent condition and Cook was in no mind to linger. They had done all that had been asked of them to do and now they were free to return to England. There were three possible routes home, so Cook called his usual democratic council of officers and, as usual, made up his mind in his own way.

They could go home by Cape Horn, but that was a long and dangerous passage. Cook doubted whether the cordage, now long past its best, could stand up to the storms they could almost certainly expect off the Cape, and food supplies, now running low, were judged insufficient for the length of the voyage and, besides, the southern winter was coming on.

They could have gone via the Cape of Good Hope, but this involved the appalling prospect of the *Endeavour*, which, at the best of times, could only sail into the wind with the greatest of difficulty, beating for endless weeks against the prevailing westerlies before reaching the Cape. This would again involve the question of food supplies. And, besides, Tasman had already done that voyage and Cook wasn't a man much given to following in the footsteps of others.

The third choice, the one Cook finally made, was the inevitable one. For Cook, it must have been irresistible, for it involved a fresh achievement, a new discovery, an exploration

77

Maori warriors drawn by Sydney Parkinson

of the only great stretch of land still left unexplored in the temperate world – the east coast of Australia. As far as Cook was aware, no European except Tasman had ever seen or set foot on the eastern side of the continent: this was a challenge after his heart. (In point of fact what Cook did not know – and died not knowing – was that he himself was the first discoverer, for neither Tasman nor he ever learned that Van Diemen's Land, which Tasman had visited, was the island we now call Tasmania and quite detached from the Australian mainland.) And when they reached the north of Australia they could head for the Dutch East Indies where, Cook knew, they could obtain provisions in quantity.

The *Endeavour* left New Zealand on 1 April. Cook's intention was to head straight for Van Diemen's Land – Tasman had left an accurate enough fix on its position – but contrary gales blew them far to the north of their intended route and when they did sight land it was Australia and not Tasmania: just as gales had caused Cook to miss the Foveaux Strait between South Island and Stewart Island, so now more gales caused him to miss Bass Strait between Australia and Tasmania. As far as Cook was concerned, he thought he'd just sighted land some way further up the same coast as Tasman had seen.

It is worth noting, perhaps, that by a remarkable coincidence Cook's attitude to the Bass Strait was as ambivalent as Tasman's to Cook Strait. Tasman, in his charts, showed North and South Islands joined together but in his journal expressed the private belief that there probably was a strait separating the two: Cook, in his chart, showed Australia and Tasmania as being joined together but in *his* journal expressed the private belief that there was probably a strait separating the two.

Almost certainly, the *Endeavour* was already in Bass Strait when Lieutenant Hicks first sighted Australia on 21 April. The location of this landfall – Point Hicks Hill – is not precisely known, but it is believed to be a hill behind a promontory now known as Cape Everard.

Cook moved along the coast, at first in an easterly then in a northerly direction, looking for a suitable harbour. They could see smoke at frequent intervals and from this they assumed that the area was inhabited although there were no people to be seen. After a week of sailing north they found what seemed an eminently suitable harbour and put into it.

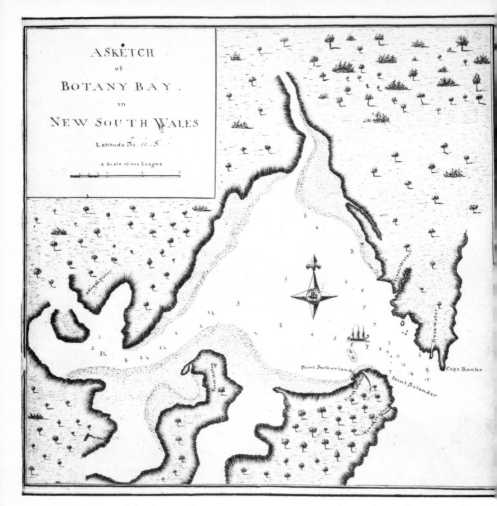

Cook's chart of Botany Bay, New South Wales, where Cook landed on 28 April 1770

Here they met their first aborigines, nearly black in colour, quite different from the Polynesians and the Maoris. Some were hostile, but not nearly as hostile as the Maoris had been. Some were indifferent – Cook relates with astonishment that two canoe-loads of aborigines, busy fishing, paid no attention whatsoever as the *Endeavour* moved in but displayed total indifference, which one cannot regard as other than totally astonishing as it was quite impossible that they had ever seen such a ship in their lives before. None of the aborigines offered any kind of welcome. All of them, it was observed, carried 'short scimitars' – the famous boomerangs.

Water was obtainable and the bay teemed with fish, to such an extent that Cook called the place Stingray Harbour, but there was no meat to be had, no fresh fruit and no vegetables – the aborigines knew nothing of the art of cultivation, which clearly made them a much more backward race than the Maoris of the Bay of Plenty, who had developed the art to a considerable degree. But one thing did abound in a profusion that delighted the hearts of Banks, Solander and the other scientists – plants. They found hundreds there that were totally unknown in Europe, so many in fact that Cook was constrained to change his mind about Stingray Harbour and give it instead that name that was to be the most famous – and with the introduction of the convict settlements, the most infamous – in early Australian history: Botany Bay.

They sailed on 6 May. About nine miles to the north they passed the entrance to another harbour, which Cook called Port Jackson, hazarding the opinion that it might prove a safe anchorage. It is as well, perhaps, for Cook's peace of mind that he died without knowing that he had just passed up the most magnificent harbour in the world: Sydney.

For the next five weeks the *Endeavour* sailed up the coast in remarkably fine weather. Cook was in his element. He had his difficulties to cope with, of course, such as when someone cut off part of the ears of his clerk, Mr Orton, when he was in a drunken stupor (the culprit was never discovered) and, later, when coping with the mazy intricacies, the rocks and shoals and reefs too innumerable to count, of the Great Barrier Reef. But in the main he was doing what he best loved to, making a splendid series of charts and christening everything in sight – the numbers of isles, bays, sounds, heads and capes that Cook named is almost beyond belief. It is another facet of his character that he must have had a remarkably inventive mind: he never once seems to have been at a loss for a name.

At 11 p.m. on the night of 11 June the *Endeavour* grounded on an underwater coral reef with an impact that shook every timber in the ship. She was held there, fast, immovable, and it was immediately apparent that the damage was of a very serious nature for great amounts of water at once started gushing into the stricken ship. To make matters worse, she had not only grounded on the top of the tide – a circumstance which ships' captains dread above all others – but the heavy swell beyond the reef was breaking as it crossed the reef and was continually pounding the stranded vessel – not heavily, but severely enough to increase the risk of extending the damage already sustained to the bottom.

The pumps were manned but could not cope with the inflow of water. As the tide receded the *Endeavour* developed a list, which put a further strain on the already damaged timbers. The more the tide went out, the greater the angle of list became. The mainland was twenty miles away. A sudden storm and the ship might be torn off the rocks tearing more timbers in the process, and founder: and there weren't enough boats to carry the complement of the vessel to safety.

It had all the makings of a desperate situation, but such are the situations that the Captain Cooks of this world are born for. He had the ship lightened as much as possible by throwing overboard about fifty tons of material – the boatswain's and carpenter's condemned stores, firewood, stone and iron ballast from the hold, even the guns – although those were carefully buoyed for later recovery. At the same time he had anchors put aboard the pinnace, and taken and dropped some distance from the *Endeavour* so that with the aid of capstan and windlass they could kedge the vessel into deeper water. One can imagine the sheer back-breaking labour involved in all this: the continuous pumping, the transport of the heavy anchors and, especially, the removal of the fifty tons of ballast from the hold. By eleven o'clock the following morning, the

Grevillea (*Grevillea gibbosa*) observed near the Endeavour River and drawn by Sydney Parkinson

time of the next high tide, almost every man on board was in a state of exhaustion.

The tide came and went and still she was stuck fast. Cook

The Endeavour River showing the ship hauled up on the shore for fothering

retained his remarkable calm. He knew that the night tides on that coast were considerably higher than the day tides. At the same time, he did question the wisdom of trying to get her off at all – for all they knew it was only the coral reef on which the *Endeavour* rested that prevented her from sinking like a stone. Cook decided to risk it. If she started to sink quickly, he would try to kedge her back on to the reef at once; if she got off and made water only comparatively slowly, he would try to sail her to the coast, beach her there, break her up and build a smaller boat from her timbers and sail in that to the East Indies. 'Indomitable' is hardly a word

that one would apply to Captain Cook if one could find a better one.

In the event, neither of those courses had to be followed. At high tide that night, with every possible hand on the windlasses attached to the anchor ropes – and most of the others at the pumps – the *Endeavour* was pulled clear. To the astonishment – and relief – of all, not only did she not sink, she now made even less water than she had done before. (What had happened, as they discovered later, was that a large chunk of coral had broken off as she'd been hauled free and had partially plugged the hole.)

Cook decided to plug the hole some more – to fother it, as it was called. A rope was passed under the ship and attached to a sail which was covered with oakum and wool. This was pulled under the ship and when it came to the hole water pressure jammed it in position, an operation which reduced incoming water to a relative trickle, although the pumps still had to be manned.

Cook dispatched boats to reconnoitre the coast to find a suitable spot where the *Endeavour* could be careened and the gash in the bottom repaired. And now luck had turned to Cook's side, for a boat returned saying that it had found a suitable river estuary on the coast, some little way to the north. Cook took the *Endeavour* there and despite the fact that he had to wait three days, because of adverse winds, to enter the river, and even then grounded twice, eventually they found a perfect anchorage not more than twenty feet from the river-bank.

Cook had the ship lightened of all stores and ballast to enable her to be warped as far as possible up the beach. The damage was serious enough – much of the underwater sheathing had been stripped off and four planks were gone, but there was nothing the resourceful carpenters and black-smiths couldn't cope with: their greatest difficulty was that they could work only at low tide when the timbers were exposed.

Here, for the first time, they managed to establish a degree of rapport with the aborigines. They were, unlike the Polynesians, a shy, reserved, almost timorous people al-though they did share to a marked degree the Tahitians' predilection for lifting things that didn't belong to them. Materially, Cook reckoned, they were the poorest people on earth – they had almost literally nothing: but Cook was astute enough to suggest that they probably led happier and more carefree lives than Europeans did.

This semi-tropical region – it must be remembered that Cook was now only fifteen degrees from the Equator – was a naturalist's joy. It teemed with wild life and fish of all kinds. Mussels and turtles there were in abundance. There were scores of tropical varieties of birds. Here they saw their first crocodiles, their first flying foxes, their first dingoes, their first wallabies, their first kangeroos.

The scientists would dearly have loved to remain there for

Banks and his colleagues saw many plants and animals for the first time, including the kangaroo, here sketched by Sydney Parkinson

an indefinite period but Cook would have none of it. Although the *Endeavour* had been well enough patched up, she was still in a basically unsatisfactory state and the nearest shipyard facilities were at Batavia, Java, in the Dutch East Indies – and Cook didn't even know how to get there for there was as yet no proof that a passage existed between Northern Australia and New Guinea. Further, he had only three months provisions left. Worst of all, if he delayed too long, the south-east trades would change to the north-west trades and it would take the *Endeavour* for ever to battle her way to Batavia against a head wind. So Cook left on 6 August, having named their temporary port the Endeavour River. (The city that now stands on that site is called Cook-town.)

They moved on north – but very circumspectly indeed. There were more shoals, reefs, rocks and islets than ever. It took Cook a whole week to get through a particularly bad section which he christened the Labyrinth. The dangers were so great that at nigh-time it was impossible to move at all. During the day, the pinnace, constantly sounding, went ahead of the *Endeavour* while on the ship Cook himself was at the mast-head, guiding and instructing all day long.

Even after the Labyrinth had been safely traversed, Cook's troubles with the Barrier Reef continued for over another week. At one point, thoroughly exasperated with the painfully slow progress they were making – it took them sixteen days to cover what a modern ship would easily do in one, although it has to be borne in mind of course that Cook was the first man ever to navigate through those infinitely treacherous seas – he took advantage of a gap in the Barrier Reef and broke through to the open ocean beyond.

But the distance between the land and the Barrier Reef steadily began to widen – the Reef kept steadily north while the land was now tending west of north. Cook became acutely unhappy. Not only was he not now in a position to

An oil painting by Webber showing Cook's men hunting sea
lions in the Arctic

William Hodges's impression of Tahitian war canoes

A watercolour of the *Resolution* by midshipman Henry Roberts

chart the course, but, much more seriously, if he stood too far out to sea and if there really was a strait between Australia and New Guinea he might miss it altogether and find himself sailing somewhere off the shores of New Guinea. Cook had no option. He turned and headed back in through the Great Barrier Reef – and in the process he almost lost the *Endeavour* on another coral reef.

However, his troubles on those, the worst and most hazardous waters he had ever encountered or was to encounter, were almost over. He closed in on land and eventually it could be seen from the mast-head that the mainland on the left had become so narrow that the sea could be seen on the other side. A little longer and there was no land at all on the port side. Cook had reached the northernmost tip of Australia and through a strait which he now named the Endeavour Strait had found a passageway through to the East Indies.

To this Cape he gave the name of Cape York: the same name has since been given to the entire peninsula. There was one last thing that Cook did not neglect to do before he left Australia, just as he hadn't neglected to perform this duty in New Zealand and many Pacific islands: he took formal and ceremonial possession of it in the name of the crown. 'New South Wales' he called it and referred to the eastern part of the Australian continent: in effect, he was claiming it all. It is rather a staggering thought that in the space of a few short months one man should add both New Zealand and Australia to the British crown.

Instead of heading directly for Batavia, Cook had to satisfy his insatiable curiosity and go and see for himself how far New Guinea lay to the north of Cape York – it had to be remembered that no one in the western world had known until then whether Australia and New Guinea were one or not. More accurately, it is believed that some knew that Torres had indeed found a strait between New Guinea and Australia but were keeping the knowledge to themselves. One of those was reported to be Alexander Dalrymple who had hoped to command the *Endeavour* himself and achieve fame by finding the Torres Strait. This information he had given to Banks who had passed it on to Cook who apparently distrusted the information as much as he distrusted Dalrymple. It is one of the more exquisite ironies of fate that it was to be Cook who, on his next and even greater voyage, was to demolish Dalrymple's dream of the Great Southern Continent.

Because of dangerous reefs, and waters so shallow that at times it was almost impossible to keep New Guinea in sight Cook, with his typical perseverance, finally succeeded in effecting a landing. The natives of the Gulf of Papua, however, turned out to be so uncompromisingly hostile that Cook pursued the matter no further. He headed the *Endeavour* east, traversed the lengths of the Arafura and Timor seas and stopped briefly at the island of Suva, at that time under the control of the Dutch East India Company. Here Cook was hospitably received, being permitted to buy quantities of fresh meat, fruit and vegetables. The *Endeavour* reached Java Head on 22 September, but so contrary were the winds and currents that she was unable to reach Batavia until 10 October, the first civilised town they had seen since leaving Rio de Janeiro almost two years previously.

Cook had already collected all the journals and diaries of his officers and men and these, along with his own journals and the many charts he had drawn, he dispatched to the Admiralty in London by means of a Dutch ship, the *Kronenburg*. Cook's covering letter makes rather astonishing reading. Although he had no illusions as to the value of his charts – 'the latitude and longitude of few parts of the world are better settled than these' – he is most extraordinarily deprecating about the importance of his discoveries. He seems almost apologetic about his failure to discover the Great Southern Continent and, as for his other activities, he says: 'The discoveries made in this voyage are not great', a quite re-markable statement from a man who had just annexed New Zealand and Australia for the British crown.

Cook, in his letter, is most complimentary about all his officers and men and equally so about the scientists. In the nature of things there must have been some who were less than perfect but Cook makes no mention of them: it is a mark of the man's fundamental generosity of nature. In all his letters Cook permitted himself the expression of only one small piece of self-satisfaction: 'I have the satisfaction to say that I have not lost one man by sickness during the whole voyage'.

That was true. If one does not include epilepsy and alcoholic poisoning under the normal definition of sickness, then his statement is accurate – the others who had died had been drowned or perished from exposure, compounded by the consumption of large quantities of rum, in the snows of Tierra del Fuego. But that ever so slightly self-satisfied statement must remain as the saddest sentence that Cook ever wrote. From the health point of view, his troubles were only then beginning: it is ironic to reflect that after this epic world-girdling voyage he arrived in Batavia, that first outpost of civilization, with all his crew in perfect health, and yet when the *Endeavour* sailed from there it did so in the condition of a hospital ship.

Batavia (since the Dutch lost control of the East Indies after the Second World War the town has been known as Djakarta) was at that time almost certainly the most unhealthy place in the world. The Dutch had built it on a flat low-lying plain after the model of one of their cities in Holland – almost every main street had its own canal running alongside it. But what worked in the cool northern climes of Amsterdam did not work in the steamy, enervated air of the tropics. The canals were filthy beyond belief, full of every imaginable type of refuse and sewage and were quite stagnant. They were

The City of BATAVIA in the Island of Java and Capital of all the Dutch Factories & Settlements in the East Indies.

Ryne delin   *Publish'd accor*

London Printed for Rob!

A view of Batavia (modern Djakarta) in 1754; in Cook's time one of the unhealthiest places on earth, as Cook's crew discovered at great cost

La Ville de BATAVIA en l'Isle de Java et Capitale de tous les
— Comptoirs et Etablissements Hollandois dans les Indes Orientales

therefore the ideal breeding ground for mosquitoes, germs and viruses of a large – and largely lethal – number of tropical diseases. Malaria, naturally, was everywhere, but dysentery appears to have been the chief killer. Banks maintains – and we have no reason to disbelieve him, he had an accurate and scientific mind – that out of every hundred troops who came out from Holland for garrison duty fifty would be dead at the end of the year, twenty-five in hospital and not more than ten fully fit for duty. Such appalling figures seem quite incredible but no less a person than Cook himself bears him out: when he left Batavia, Dutch captains told him that he, Cook, could consider himself very lucky that half his crew were not dead.

When, repairs completed, the *Endeavour* sailed from Batavia just after Christmas, she had already lost seven of her complement and over forty were so seriously ill that they were unable to help work the ship. And the rest of the crew, Cook wrote, were in poor condition. The seven who died were the surgeon himself, Tupia and his servant, the astronomer Green's servant, and three seamen. Banks became critically ill and saved himself only by taking to the cooler and fresher air of the mountains and dosing himself with large quantities of quinine.

When Cook left Batavia for Cooktown he must – one assumes – have done so with heartfelt relief, confident that the worst lay behind. But the horrifying worst was yet to come. The journals for that ten-week trip between Batavia and the Cape of Good Hope make appalling reading. Four weeks out from Batavia a marine died, and within the next week ten more had died also, including Green, the astronomer, and Parkinson, the natural history draughtsman. In the following month of February twelve more members of the crew died which meant that in that one – comparatively – brief voyage from the Indies to Africa one-quarter of the original ship's company died. At one particularly desperate stage in that voyage there were only twelve people fit to work the ship and even they were in a poor state of health.

Cook himself appears to have remained marvellously immune to sickness and this may well have been the case: he does appear to have been possessed of an iron constitution. Equally well, he too may have been ill, but neither shown it nor mentioned it: when he had his right hand almost blown off by a gun-powder flask when surveying the Newfoundland coast or, later, when he was critically ill with a gall-bladder infection, he does not at any time refer to his own sufferings.

The *Endeavour* arrived at Cape Town on 14 March. Those who were still very seriously ill – there were about thirty of them – were put ashore to hospital. That meant that Cook was now without half his original crew and that there were less than twenty left aboard capable of working the ship. Fortunately Cook was able to engage fresh crew in Cape Town to help him sail the *Endeavour* back to England.

Three more of the *Endeavour's* crew died while in hospital. In mid-April, Cook brought his sick aboard and sailed for England: some were still very ill men indeed, one to such an extent that he died even before they cleared Table Bay. On the way home Lieutenant Hicks also died – he had been a consumptive for a long time. And then on 12 July 1771, two years and eleven months after sailing, the *Endeavour* was home again.

CHAPTER 5

ANTARCTICA AND POLYNESIA

I T would be pleasant to record that on his return to England Cook found himself to be the hero of the hour. This does not seem to have been the case. As far as the general public and the Royal Society were concerned, Banks and Solander were the people who really mattered. It was they who had brought back all the evidences and proofs and souvenirs of those exotic and glamorous lands at the other end of the earth, all the trophies, all the skins of animals and birds of which the world had known nothing, fish which had never been seen before, countless numbers of unknown insects and hundreds of preserved plants unknown in Europe: it was reckoned that the unfortunate Parkinson, the natural history artist, had completed over 1,500 drawings and sketches of unknown flora and fauna before his death. And there can be no doubt that Banks and his scientists deserved all praise: under the most arduous conditions they had performed splendidly and their achievements in opening up fresh avenues in natural history have been surpassed, perhaps, only by Darwin. So it was perhaps understandable that Banks and his friends basked in the limelight while Cook was largely regarded as the person who had chauffeured them from place to place.

In addition, of course, the reception accorded them depended upon their natures. Banks, a wealthy young socialite with a host of influential friends, loved to be lionised. Cook, rather withdrawn, rather remote, a passio-

Sir Joseph Banks, surrounded by trophies from his voyages, and at the time of this painting President of the Royal Society

nate defender of his own privacy, avoided the blaze of publicity wherever possible. Cook, clearly, was indifferent to popular acclaim. He had set out to achieve something, he had achieved it and that was all the reward that he would ever wish for.

But, even for Cook, it must have been extremely gratifying that what acclaim did come his way came from professionals, the only people really capable of appreciating the magnitude of his achievements. The Lords of the Admiralty, customarily a reticent and unforthcoming body when it came to bestowing a due meed of approbation, heaped upon Cook a degree of praise so extravagant that Cook must have found it slightly embarrassing. In fact, the praise only seemed to be extravagant: given Cook's achievements, no praise could have been too high.

There can be no question but that his superiors now regarded Cook as the greatest explorer and navigator of his age. There is no question that Cook's obscure origins and long years before the mast had been completely forgotten and that he was now one of 'them', an intimate and genuine friend of those who walked the corridors of naval power. But, at the same time – and this without in any way being cynical – it has to be borne in mind that Cook was now the biggest public relations asset that the Navy had had in generations and that, moreover, the extraordinary successes he had achieved redounded mightily on the perspicacity and farsightedness of those who had picked the right man for that great task – their Lordships themselves.

Such a tremendous asset as this could not be allowed to rust in disuse. Immediately after his return Cook was promoted to Commander and given the command of *H.M.S. Scorpion*. Clearly, the Admiralty had no intention that Cook should ever sail aboard her: it was merely a holding appointment, a device whereby Cook was retained at full pay while being free to devote himself to a vastly more important matter: preparation for a new expedition to the South Seas.

It is not quite certain who was the moving spirit or what was the prime motivation behind this second expedition. A certain degree of vagueness surrounds the inception of the idea. Some such projects appear to grow out of nothing, then become gradually, vaguely talked about, then are bruited abroad and achieve a certain degree of definition and then, suddenly, find a broad overall degree of acceptance and the idea becomes reality. Certainly, the Royal Society had a hand in it – they regarded themselves as a semi-governmental body and were a powerful force in the Establishment. Certainly, Cook himself would have been far from passive in the matter: like all great explorers, once he had savoured the joys and satisfactions of penetrating the unknown, he could never rest until he was on his way again. Certainly the leading geographers of the day, notably Alexander Dalrymple who still clung tenaciously to his idea of a Southern Continent, would have pressed for this second expedition. But one feels that the real decision-makers in this case were the Lords of the Amiralty.

Perhaps they had in mind the possibility that Cook might indeed stumble upon this mythical Southern Continent, or on some other country or island so far undiscovered, and annex it with his customary speed for the British crown: an intriguingly pleasant thought and not an impossibilty, for the southern seas was still a vast unknown: apart from the occasions when he had rounded the Horn and South Island, New Zealand, Cook had hardly once gone beyond latitude 40° south. It is more likely that they said to Cook, in effect, that he should embark upon another epic voyage of discovery – it wouldn't matter particularly where he went – that would bring fresh credit and honour and glory to himself and his country and, incidentally, to their Lordships of the Admiralty.

In support of this contention it must be pointed out that Cook received no specific instructions for this second voyage, the most awesome ever undertaken. Parenthetically, it may be observed that no one would ever undertake such a voyage again for when Cook had finished with the high latitudes of the southern oceans, on this voyage that was to last over three years, there was precious little left for anyone else to discover.

There is no doubt that Cook was given complete *carte blanche* as to where he should go and what he should do. This can be proven. In the journal of his first voyage Cook wrote:

I hope it will not be taken amiss if I give it as my opinion that the most feasible method of making further discoveries in the South Sea is to enter by way of New Zealand, first touching at the Cape of Good Hope: from thence proceed to the southward of New Holland for Queen Charlotte Sound, where again refresh wood and water, taking care to be ready to leave that place by the latter end of September, or beginning of October at the furthest, when you would have the whole summer before you and after getting through the Strait, might, with the prevailing Westerly winds, run to the Eastward in as high a latitude as you please and if you meet with no lands would have time enough to get round Cape Horn before the summer was too far spent: but if after meeting with no Continent, and you had other objects in view, then haul to the Northward, and after visiting some islands already discovered, after which proceed with the trade winds back to the Westward in search of those before mentioned – thus the discoveries of the South Sea would be complete.

(There is some slight confusion at the beginning of this excerpt. What Cook means is that the next expedition should go to Cape Town and then directly to Cook Strait in New Zealand from where it would leave for Antarctic waters.)

As this is precisely the basic route that Cook was to follow there is no question but that the Admiralty were in total agreement with him. They also readily acceded to Cook's two further demands: that he should have a larger vessel than

I received a commission to comand His
Majestys Sloop Drake at this time in the Dock at
Deptford, Burthen 462 Tons to be mand with 110
Men including officers & to carry twelve guns at
the same time Captain Tobias Furneaux was
appointed to the command of the Raleigh at Woolwich
Burthen 336 Tons, 80 Ment & ten guns. These two Sloops
were both built at Whitby by Mr Fishburn the same
as built the Endeavour Bark, the former about
fourteen and the latter eighteen Months ago, and had
just been purchased into the Navy from Cap. William
Hammond of Hull in order to be sent on discoveries to
the South Sea under my directions. The Admiralty
gave orders that they sould be fitted in the best manner
possible, the Earl of Sandwich at this time first Lord
intrested himself very much in the Equipment and he
was
well seconded by Mr Pallisor and Sr Jn. Williams
the one Comptroller and the other Surveyor of the
Navy, the Victualling Board was also very attentive
in procuring the very best of every kind of Provisions
in short every department seemd to vie with each other
in equiping these two Sloops; every standing Rule and
order in the Navy was dispensed with; every alteration
every necessary and usefull article was granted as soon
as asked for——
Two days after I received my Commission I hoisted the
Pendant and took charge of the Sloop accordingly
and began to enter Seamen the Vestal Frigate at this
time in ordinary, was appointed to receive them untill
the Sloop came out of Dock——
The Admiralty changed the Sloops Names to.
Resolution and Adventure and the officers
were ordered to take out new Comissions & Warrants
accordingly——

A painting by Francis Holman done in 1771 and showing the *Resolution* and the *Adventure*, the two ships in which Cook's second expedition set sail from Plymouth in July 1772

the *Endeavour*, which he had found too cramped; and that, for safety's sake and mutual comfort and support, a second vessel should accompany him.

As Cook had found the *Endeavour*, size apart, eminently

suitable for his purposes, two more Whitby collier-type vessels were purchased by the Admiralty: the *Marquis of Granby*, 462 tons and a complement of 118 men and the *Marquis of Rockingham*, 350 tons and a complement of 83. On transfer to the Navy they were commissioned under the names of *Drake* and *Raleigh*; but wiser thoughts prevailed. The Spanish still had considerable pretensions in the Pacific –

not to put too fine a point upon it they regarded it as their own private property – and it was felt, and rightly, that those two names might give almost as much offence to the Spanish as Drake and Raleigh had given to the Spanish almost two centuries previously. So they were re-named *Resolution* and *Adventure*.

Cook was to have as his First Lieutenant a certain Lieutenant Cooper – a relation of Cook's old mentor Palliser – and Lieutenants Pickersgill and Clerke, both of whom had sailed with himself in the *Endeavour* and with Wallis in the *Dolphin*. They were now about to make their third circumnavigation of the world so Cook had no lack of experienced assistance. The *Adventure* was to be captained by a certain Tobias Furneaux, a very experienced officer who had already been around the world with Wallis. His senior lieutenants were called Shank and Kempe.

It was proposed that Banks and an entourage of scientists and servants should again join this expedition. It is variously claimed that the proposal came from the Earl of Sandwich (then First Lord), the Royal Society and Banks himself. It hardly matters: Banks, with his wealth and far-ranging connections with the establishment of the day, was an extremely influential young man and was accepted.

Alas, Banks' long period of lionization in the very best of London society appeared to have had a considerable effect on his powers of judgment. He adopted from the outset the attitude that Cook would be little more than his, Banks', ocean-going chauffeur and that he, Banks, would direct the voyage, both as to where they went and how long they should remain in any particular place. Moreover, he wanted to bring along a party of no less than fifteen, including a couple of horn-players for his own special edification. Finally, when he saw the *Resolution*, he pronounced it unfit for a gentleman to embark upon. He had the effrontery to suggest that a larger vessel be provided, a suggestion that the Admiralty, under-

Tobias Furneaux, who captained the *Adventure*. Furneaux came from Devon and as second lieutenant had sailed with Wallis on the *Dolphin*

standably enough, dismissed out of hand. He then proposed that the Great Cabin on the *Resolution* should be enlarged and a false deck built aft over the existing deck in order to provide him, his entourage and their masses of scientific equipment all the room they required. In this the Admiralty, astonishingly, acquiesced.

While those alterations were taking place Cook, in addition to overseeing all the preparations for the expedition and recruiting crews for the voyage, was having troubles of his own. An official version of his journals of the *Endeavour* was being prepared but it wasn't Cook who was preparing them. As a simple, rough sailor it was thought that Cook was unfitted for so literary a task so a leading light of the literary establishment and crony of Dr Johnson, a certain Dr John Hawkesworth, was brought in to apply the necessary polish: he was either brought in or he wangled the commission for himself and if the latter were the case then at the fee of £6,000 for the job, a fortune in those days, it was a pretty fair piece of wangling.

Hawkesworth was a pedantic idiot with an unbridled imagination, and the end result of his labours was a travesty of what Cook had written. Cook, admittedly, was consulted freely and frequently, but Hawkesworth paid no attention to what he said, edited the journals as he saw fit, ignored Cook's protests and gave him no opportunity to revise or edit it before publication: fortunately for Cook, he was at sea before the book was published. In the passing, it might be mentioned that a certain Dr Beaglehole brought out an unexpurgated version of Cook's own journals some years ago. It is so incomparably better a book that it seems unlikely that anyone except a professional historian would ever take the trouble to read Hawkesworth's book again.

At the same time, Cook was having trouble with the Royal Society who professed themselves disappointed in the results of the Venus transit. Most of their criticisms, it is true, were levelled at Green, but as Green was now dead Cook felt himself called upon to defend him and did so with such anger and such bitterness that his reply had to be omitted from the official copy of the Journal.

Meanwhile, the alterations to the *Resolution* had been completed. Their effects upon the stability and sea-keeping qualities of the *Resolution* were totally disastrous. She was so impossibly top-heavy that she was in danger of capsizing even in a relatively calm sea. Her pilot down the Thames refused to put on all sail lest she went over and said he'd be damned if he'd take her further than the Nore. Lieutenant Clerke, who shared this rather daunting experience, wrote: 'By God, I'll go to sea in a grog-tub, if required, or in the *Resolution*, as soon as you please: but must say I think her by far the most unsafe ship I ever saw or heard of'.

The Admiralty clearly thought so also for they ordered her back to dock and had all the newly added superstructure removed. It is reported that Banks, upon seeing this, 'swore and stamped upon the wharf like a madman', had all his gear removed, and wrote furiously to the Admiralty roundly condemning them for their action and asking that a larger ship should be provided at once. The Admiralty, clearly, had had enough of Banks, his importunities and his far from incipient delusions of grandeur, pointing out to him that this expedition was not being mounted for his sole benefit and that if he thought it was and that he was to be the director and conductor of the whole then he was gravely in error. Banks left in a huff for a private expedition to Iceland. It is interesting, however, that it did not alter the friendship that existed between Cook and himself: when Cook returned from his second voyage no one welcomed him more warmly and enthusiastically than Banks.

The scientists and artists who had departed *en masse* with Banks had to be replaced. The scientists were to be led by a distinguished German naturalist, John Reinhold Forster (he was of Scottish descent, hence the name), a cantankerous and petty-minded prude who complained about everything and everybody from the moment he came on board. But he *was* good, no doubt about that. With him was his son, George, a much more likeable character, who was to be the natural history draughtsman. A William Hodges was employed as a

John Reinhold Forster (holding a bird) and his son George. Forster senior was not a popular member of the expedition but he was a competent scientist and was able to collect a lot of entirely new information about the flora and fauna of the Pacific Islands

landscape painter, and a very successful one he proved to be, and an astronomer from the Board of Longitude, a certain William Wales who, along with Cook, was to check the efficacy of a new type of chronometer in determining longitude at sea. (Another astronomer, William Bayly, was aboard the *Adventure* for the same purpose.)

On 13 July, a year and a day after Cook had arrived back in the *Endeavour*, the *Resolution* and the *Adventure* sailed from Plymouth.

The journey south to Cape Town was comparatively un-eventful. Cook lost one man overboard, while Furneaux lost a couple of midshipmen as a result of fever contracted when they made a stop at the Cape Verde Islands. (They had made an earlier stop at Madeira to pick up fresh fruit and vegetables and, of course, large stocks of Madeira wine.)

Cape Town was reached on 30 October. To Cook's chagrin, stores that had been ordered well in advance had not yet arrived and he had to wait just over a month before sailing. While he was there he heard news of the activities of French ships in the Indian Ocean and the Pacific. Two vessels out from Mauritius, had allegedly discovered land due south of Mauritius – which it wasn't – on the 48th parallel south, which it was. Two other French vessels, under a certain Marion du Fresne, had arrived in New Zealand in March 1772. In June their leader was killed by the Maoris in the Bay of Plenty and the French left for home, having named it Austral-France and having claimed it on behalf of the King of France, quite unaware that Cook had done the same thing in the name of England's king some two years previously. But they did not circumnavigate and chart the island as Cook had done.

While in Cape Town, the Forsters met a renowned Swedish botanist, a former pupil of Linnaeus called Anders Sparrman, and they asked Cook's permission to have him along. Cook gave his consent. It says much for the carefree attitude adopted to travel in those days that a man busily botanising in Cape Town should more or less casually step aboard a vessel which, he has been warned in advance, will not touch civilization again for at least two years.

Completely provisioned for a long stay at sea – the cargo now included a considerable amount of mixed livestock for

A painting by George Forster of the *Felix capensis* (Cape cat); now called Felis serval, or large spotted serval

distribution through the various Pacific islands – the two ships put to sea on 22 November. Cook's first intention was to try to locate an island rejoicing in the odd name of Cape Circumcision. At least, Cook thought that it would be an island: it could, of course, have been a promontory of the fabled Southern Continent. It was reputed to be about 1,700 miles south of the Cape of Good Hope and had been sighted by a Captain Bouvet who was known to be a reliable observer: and it was just possible that this might be in some way connected with the recent discovery of Kerguelen's Island which was in roughly the same latitudes but some considerable way to the east – perhaps they were both part of the Southern Continent.

Cook never did find Cape Circumcision and it is hardly to be wondered at that he failed. It does in fact exist – it is today known as Bouvet Island – but it is the tiniest imaginable spot in the immensity of the south Atlantic. For two or three

A painting by George Forster of the *Yerbua capensis*, another Cape animal; now called Pedetes cafer, or Spring-haas

weeks, in bitter weather and gale force seas, Cook quartered the area searching for this elusive place and finally came to the conclusion that it didn't exist. It is quite clear that whatever navigational fixes Cook had been given on this island must have been wildly wrong, for there is no doubt that with

Chronometer made by Larcum Kendall in 1769. Cook found it very reliable and used it during his second voyage for fixing longitude

the aid of the new and exceptionally accurate Kendall chronometers he had with him, Cook could have pin-pointed even the smallest island in the Atlantic with complete precision. However, Cook did not feel that his time here had been at all

A watercolour by Sydney Parkinson of *Aechmea nudicaulis*, a
plant collected by Banks and Solander in Rio de Janeiro in 1768

Banksia (*Banksia intergrifolia*) observed near the Endeavour River and painted by Sydney Parkinson

wasted: if nothing else he had established that no portion of the Southern Continent existed in those parts.

Even though it was then just approaching high summer in those latitudes, the cold was already severe, the men were in their Fearnoughts again, the livestock was dying because of the low temperatures and, about mid-December, the first of the icebergs put in an appearance. Cook decided to cast around once more for this elusive island and then give up the search.

Christmas Day was cold but the weather conditions were good. The crew, as Cook dryly observes, 'were inclinable to celebrate the day in their own way, for which purpose they had been hoarding up liquor for some time, I also made some addition to their allowance . . . mirth and good-humour ranged throughout the ship'. John Forster's comment – 'savage noise and drunkenness'.

Early in January, having abandoned all hope of finding Bouvet's land, Cook turned the ships first south-east and then south, down towards the Antarctic regions to make the first really deeply penetrating probe in search of Dalrymple's unknown continent. There were icebergs everywhere, wondrous floating islands that reached higher than the masts of the ships, islands tinted with the most extraordinary range of pastel colours, mostly blues and greens, though some were mauve and pinkish in appearance: some of those icebergs were quite small, no larger than the ships: others were as much as two miles in diameter. Provided visibility wasn't obscured by snow or fog, the icebergs presented no real danger as at that time of year in those high latitudes there was enough light to see by twenty-four hours a day – no danger, that is, if ships didn't sail too close to them: as the icebergs drifted further north, the submerged parts became eaten away by the relatively warmer water and it quite often happened that, because of this under-water erosion, an iceberg would suddenly lose its stability and fall over on its

An engraving based on a drawing by William Hodges of the crew
of the *Resolution* collecting ice for drinking water (as observed by
Hodges on 9 January 1773)

side. It behoved a prudent captain to be nowhere in the vicinity when any such thing occurred.

Shortage of fresh water was now becoming a problem and the simple answer to this was to obtain it from the ice. When they encountered an ice-field made up of pieces of ice of manageable size, boats would be lowered and ice brought back to the ship – Cook mentions as much as fifteen tons having being brought aboard at one time. When melted, this ice proved to contain no salt whatsoever but it was obviously different from ordinary water inasmuch as everybody who used it was afflicted by a swelling of the glands of the throat. It was Forster's opinion, and he was probably correct, that this was due to the fact that the ice held no trace of the free oxygen which is a constituent of normal water.

On 17 January 1773, the ships crossed the Antarctic Circle, the first vessel ever known to do so. The very next day they encountered their first field of pack-ice – that is to say, ice that has been formed by the freezing of the surface of the sea as distinct from iceberg ice which comes from glaciers on land. This pack-ice, soon stretching all the way across the horizon, became so thick as to make any further progress impossible. Cook headed north again, well enough satisfied: if Dalrymple's Southern Continent did exist then it was steadily shrinking in size.

Early in February, *Resolution* and *Adventure* were cruising about in the relatively mild climate and warm waters of 48° south, searching for Kerguelen's island. The search, and it was an intensive one, yielded nothing which, in retrospect, is less than surprising for Cook was looking in quite the wrong place. He had been given the correct latitude – 48° south – but the longitudinal bearings were very far out. Cook had been told that Kerguelen Island lay due south of Mauritius, and he knew that the longitude of Mauritius was 57° 30′ east. Kerguelen Island, in fact, is 70° east, so Cook was carrying out his search hundreds of miles to the westward of Kerguelen's actual position.

The weather conditions were now extreme. There was a constant succession of violent gales from the south-west and the two Whitby colliers took fearful punishment from the great seas. In the few, the very few lulls between gales, the vessels were plagued by dense fog and it was in one such fog, on 8 February, that *Resolution* and *Adventure* lost contact with each other. For three days, as by pre-arrangement, the *Resolution* cruised around, firing off a signal gun at hourly intervals during the day and burning flares at night. But they failed to find the *Adventure*. Cook was not perturbed. He had anticipated that such a thing might well happen and had arranged a rendezvous in Queen Charlotte Sound in New Zealand. He had no worries on the score of the *Adventure* getting there – Tobias Furneaux was an excellent seaman and navigator.

The weather conditions were so vile that the most obvious and easiest thing for Cook to have done was to take advantage of the powerful south-westerlies and run straight for Cook Strait in New Zealand: but when Cook was bent on exploration the easy and the obvious did not exist for him. He turned the *Resolution* south-east and headed for polar waters again. The weather continued to be uniformly dreadful and Cook did not dare take his ship as far south as he had on 17 January (incidentally, had he been able to do so in those particular longitudes, he could well have discovered Antarctica for, in this area, part of Wilkes Land lies to the north of the Antarctic Circle).

Instead, Cook cruised – if that is the word, considering the abominable weather conditions – east for about three weeks, roughly on the 60th parallel, although on one occasion he reached 62° south, which took him within three hundred miles of Wilkes Land. (He had been much closer to the Antarctic continent on 17 January.) During this period no land of any kind, not even the most insignificant island was seen: there was nothing but this eternal waste of icy, storm-plagued waters. It was not until 17 March that Cook headed the *Resolution* north-east for New Zealand. He was well content. True, he had discovered nothing, but he had established one incontrovertible fact: wherever the Great Southern Continent – and if it did exist it was steadily becoming less great – lay, it most certainly did not lie in the southern latitudes between South Africa and New Zealand. Speaking roughly, then, Cook had established that the Southern Continent did not lie in the region of the south Indian Ocean: what he had yet to ascertain was whether or not it might lie in the South Pacific or the South Atlantic. It has to be constantly borne in mind, in order to appreciate the tremendous scope and sweep of Cook's achievements, that no one before had ever explored the far southern waters of the Indian Ocean *or* the Pacific *or* the Atlantic. Cook was to do all three in this one stupendous voyage. And this, it should be noted, was in addition to the two sweeps he carried out through the Central Pacific itself. The first, and much the smaller of those, was still on such a scale that it would easily have encompassed a land the size of Australia. The scope of the second sweep, which was to take him from deep in the Antarctic almost to the equator, and for many thousands of miles from New Zealand to the east of Easter Island, is of such a scale as to be barely comprehensible: certainly, it was the greatest exploratory voyage of its kind ever undertaken in the Pacific.

It had been Cook's original intention to go directly to Cook Strait and rendezvous with Furneaux in Queen Charlotte Sound, but he changed his mind and headed for the first safe and available anchorage – Dusky Sound in the south-west tip of South Island, which he'd noted on his first circumnavigation of the island. His ostensible reason was that he wanted to examine the area's natural resources and estimate the Sound's potential as a port. His true reason was almost certainly to allow his crew to rest and recuperate. Behind them lay a voyage of 117 days – almost four moths – during which they had seen no sight of land, four months in bitter temperatures and heavy seas. John Forster, though much given to complaint even under the best of circumstances, was probably right when he described the voyage as a series of hardships such as had never been experienced before.

Six weeks later, his crew fully relaxed and fit again, Cook sailed north for his rendezvous with Furneaux whom he found taking his ease in the beautiful and placid waters of Queen Charlotte Sound, the rigging all stripped off the *Adventure* in the comfortable expectation of spending a very pleasant winter in those idyllic surroundings. Furneaux, assisted by favourable and very powerful winds, had made an extremely fast passage from where he had lost contact with Cook to Tasmania – a distance of over three thousand miles – in twenty-six days. He had sailed north along the east coast of Tasmania in order to decide, once and for all, whether or not there did exist a strait between Tasmania and Australia: for some totally incomprehensible reason he and his officers decided there was no such thing, only a very deep bay. Cook accepted his word for it and was never to go and investigate for himself: he had no reason to.

To what must have been Furneaux' considerable dismay, Cook ordered him to set about re-rigging the *Adventure* without delay. He had no intention of lazing away the winter in the Sound. They were there to explore and explore was what they were going to do, if for no other reason than to prove that exploration need not cease because of the advent of winter. The area he wished to explore lay to the east and north of New Zealand: by far the greater part of this area was still virgin territory for the explorer.

The *Resolution* and *Adventure* left Queen Charlotte Sound

on 7 June, passed out through Cook Strait and headed more or less due east for several weeks, encountering nothing. They then turned on a more northerly course, hoping to locate Pitcairn Island, which had been discovered by Carteret in 1767, but a change of plan was forced on Cook when, on 29 July, to his great dismay, he heard from Furneaux – who was himself at that time crippled with gout – that one man had died aboard the *Adventure* and that twenty were seriously ill. Cook immediately went aboard and found out that not only was this the case but that many others of the crew were in a weakly condition. To Cook's chagrin and anger, the cause was the same in every case – scurvy. The reason was simple – Furneaux just hadn't troubled to enforce the anti-scurvy diet on which Cook had insisted. It is worth noting that, at that same time, Cook did not have one sick man aboard the *Resolution*.

Cook abandoned his immediate plans for exploration and laid off a course for Tahiti. The welfare of the sick crew of the *Adventure* was of greater importance than sighting new islands and it was essential to get them to a safe and sheltered spot with all speed and the nearest such haven Cook knew of in that part of the Pacific was Tahiti.

Cook made his second landfall off Tahiti just over a fortnight later. As he was anxious to acquire fresh supplies of vegetables and fruit as quickly as was possible, he made his first stop at Vaitepiha Bay in the south-east. It was very nearly his last stop anywhere. While they lay to outside the harbour, buying fruit from the Tahitians in their canoes, the wind dropped and a powerful current swept the *Resolution* in towards a coral reef, and in spite of all that Cook and his men could do it seemed inevitable that she must strike hard on the reef: but in the last few critical moments a miraculous land breeze sprang up and took her clear of the coral. Sparrman, the Swedish botanist, marvelled at the calmness and total absence of panic among Cook and his crew even when under the most severe pressure; but he was, he said, extremely shocked by Cook's language. Another report has it that the crisis had been so severe that Cook was afterwards compelled to revive himself with brandy. It seems hardly likely.

Cook found it impossible to get any fresh meat in Vaitepiha Bay so, in company with the *Adventure*, he moved round the island and took up the *Endeavour's* old anchorage in Matavai Bay. Cook – and the fifteen officers and men who had been with him aboard the *Endeavour* – received a tumultuous welcome. Old friendships were renewed and cemented and new ones made with such briskness that we find Forster, writing of their first night there, complaining bitterly that 'A great number of women of the lowest class having been engaged by our sailors remained aboard at sunset'.

Tents were erected on the site of the former Fort Venus and the sick aboard the *Adventure* were carried, and cared for, there. Cook made certain that their diet included as much fruit and vegetables as they could consume and this treatment had a rapid and remarkable effect: within a month Cook judged that the *Adventure's* crew were fit to put to sea again, and as he had come to Tahiti in the first place only with the intent of restoring the men to health, he was, as ever, not disposed to linger.

Moreover, he wanted to be on his way for two other pressing reasons. As in Vaitepiha, so in Matavai – there was no fresh meat obtainable: the hogs that used to roam the island in such great numbers were reduced to a few dozen only. But, Cook was told, there were plentiful supplies to be obtained in Huahine and Raiatea, two islands that Cook had visited before on his first voyage. Secondly, he was concerned with the time factor. He wanted to relocate a group of islands that had been discovered by Tasman in the middle of the previous century – Tasman had given them the names of Amsterdam, Rotterdam, and Middleburg –

Odiddy, from the island of Bora Bora, who sailed with Cook as an interpreter among the islands of the Pacific. A crayon portrait by William Hodges

and then return to Queen Charlotte Sound in order to be ready to leave there in November for his summer sweep through the high latitudes.

Resolution and *Adventure* sailed at the beginning of September, fully provisioned with water, wood and as much fruit and vegetables as they could carry: they had also with them two young men to serve as interpreters, Odiddy, a man from Bora Bora, aboard the *Resolution*, and Omai, from Raiatea, aboard the *Adventure*. Again, Cook was to discover that the joy with which they came to Tahiti was sadly counter-balanced by their grief in leaving it. As before, the weeping Tahitians begged them not to go away; as before the bay was crowded with canoes crammed with lamenting Tahitians.

Their first call was at Huahine, which Cook had visited three years previously. The welcome was just as warm as it had been on the previous occasion: more importantly, they were able to obtain no fewer than three hundred hogs there so that Cook's fresh meat and salt pork problems were over for a considerable time to come. Further supplies were obtained at Raiatea so that by the time they left the Society Isles the ships were even better provisioned than they had been when they had left England.

Cook set a course slightly south of west. On 24 September they sighted two small islands which Cook did not consider worth investigating. He named them the Hervey Islands and passed on. (They are part of a much larger group now known as the Cook Islands.) On 1 October they arrived at the first of the three islands Tasman had discovered, Middleburg – a name that has now reverted to the original Eua.

Cook and his men were the first white men the inhabitants of Eua had ever seen but in so far as the attitude of the natives were concerned, Cook and his men might have been long lost relatives. Their kindness, hospitality and friendliness were overwhelming to the extent of being unbelievable.

Not even in his beloved Tahiti had Cook ever experienced anything like it in the Pacific. They were feted and dined and shown over the island. The islanders had reached, as Cook noted in his journal, a much higher state of civilisation than any other Pacific people. They were, as one crew member wrote, a beautiful people in a beautiful island. All arable land was under intensive cultivation, being squared off in neat plots with pathways intersecting them. Their houses were the most immaculate Cook had seen in the Pacific, with equally immaculate rush matting on the floors. They were a clean, healthy, happy and industrious people, generous to a fault in their trading – Cook wrote of them as being more desirous to give than to receive, a statement he had been unable to make about the natives of any other island in the Pacific. They were, the astronomer Wales wrote, the most lively, laughing creatures he had ever seen. And Cook noted, with more than mild astonishment, that not only did men and women eat together – which was forbidden in Tahiti – but the men even went to the extraordinarily gallant lengths of helping the women first.

From there they sailed to a much larger island, the one on which Tasman had landed and named Amsterdam – it has now reverted to its original name of Tongatabu. Here they received the same exceptionally friendly welcome as they had in Eua. Here they were again able to carry on a brisk trade on very advantageous terms, and here again, as in Eua, they never saw a single person carrying a weapon, although Sparrman, who appeared to be possessed of the same prudish, niggling and contentious nature as his friend Forster, did introduce a rather sour note by demanding to know why, if they were so eminently peaceful a people, did he see so many war clubs everywhere. It never occurred to Sparrman, apparently, that those clubs might have been for defensive purposes only against raiders from other islands: the islanders on Eua and Tongatabu, with their advanced and intensive systems of cultivation, were a comparatively wealthy people and must have offered a very tempting target to more impoverished tribes on neighbouring islands.

When the two ships left on 8 October, their provision holds were crammed with fruit and vegetables, while they also carried with them ⌣ live – three hundred fowls and about half that number of pigs. The thought occurs that both vessels must have sounded very like a farmyard.

Because of the wonderful hospitality they had received, Cook gave to those islands the name of the Friendly Islands but although that name is still in fairly common use today they are better – and officially – known as the Tonga Islands.

Two weeks later the ships were off Hawke's Bay on the east coast of New Zealand's North Island, taking very severe punishment from southerly and south-west gales that were making it almost impossible for them to beat their way

A painting by William Hodges of a waterspout on the New Zealand coast

southwards towards Cook Strait. Eventually, the gales developed into a full-scale storm, so severe that the *Adventure*, an even poorer sailer than the *Resolution*, was blown out to sea, Cook losing contact with her on the night of 29 October. Cook managed to fight his way round Cape Palliser, the south-east tip of North Island and the entrance to Cook Strait when, to his chagrin, the wind changed to the north-west and came howling directly down through the strait, making entrance quite impossible. Cook was blown to the south-east and then south, along the east coast of South Island for such a distance that he seriously contemplated finding a harbour there instead of going to Queen Charlotte Sound. Unfortunately, he had no option – he had to rendezvous with Furneaux there, so Cook battled north against varying head-winds until he found shelter in a harbour in the Cook Strait itself, just beyond Palliser Bay at the southern end of north island. This, had he but known, would have offered some consolation for that day in May, three and a half years previously, when he had sailed by Sydney Harbour without giving it a second glance, for now, in seeking protection from the storm, he had stumbled across the splendid harbour of Port Nicholson, on which the capital of New Zealand, Wellington, now stands.

The winds moderated and on the following day the *Resolution* put into Queen Charlotte Sound. There was no sign of the *Adventure* nor did Cook expect to find her there for some little time. They waited in the sound for about three weeks during which time they learned an interesting and highly unpleasant fact: the Maoris living there, with whom Cook and his men were on good terms, were undoubtedly cannibals for, while the English were there, the local Maori war band arrived back after a raid on their enemies in nearby Admiralty Bay bearing with them an enemy body which they proceeded to cook and eat with great relish before the horrified watchers on the *Resolution*.

At the end of those three weeks Cook decided that he could wait no longer: to penetrate any distance at all into the polar waters he had to go at high summer or not at all and if he were to delay much longer he would be too late. Accordingly, he left a note in a bottle for Furneaux saying that after he, Cook, had returned from the polar regions he would probably make for Easter Island and then Tahiti, leaving it up to Furneaux whether to return to England or to attempt to rejoin him somewhere in the Pacific – which, when one considers the sheer immensity of the Pacific and the total absence of any suggested date, makes this a very optimistic proposal indeed.

As Furneaux makes no further appearance in Cook's story, this appears the appropriate place to recount briefly what had happened to him. After he had been separated from the *Resolution* in the storm, he had been blown a considerable distance out to sea to the north and east and it had taken him some days to fight his way back to the east coast of North Island. When he did regain contact he put into Tolaga Bay – the first port that Cook had entered in New Zealand on his first voyage – for wood and water and then moved south to the rendezvous. Unfortunately, adverse winds had prevented him attempting Cook Strait until the 30 November – and Cook had left Queen Charlotte Sound on the 25th: it had been as close as that.

Furneaux anchored in Queen Charlotte Sound and spent the next two weeks carrying out repairs to the *Adventure*. Then on 16 December he sent a boat's crew consisting of two officers and eight men ashore to collect what vegetables and greens they could. They did not return. A search party that set out the following day discovered that all ten had been killed and eaten by the Maoris.

Understandably sickened by this episode, Furneaux decided to return to England. He made an extremely fast passage to the Horn – it took him just over a month – and then stopped over at Cape Town before making his way back to England.

Cook, on leaving Queen Charlotte Sound, sailed south for about ten days before altering his course to the south-east: after a week on this course the first icebergs were encountered

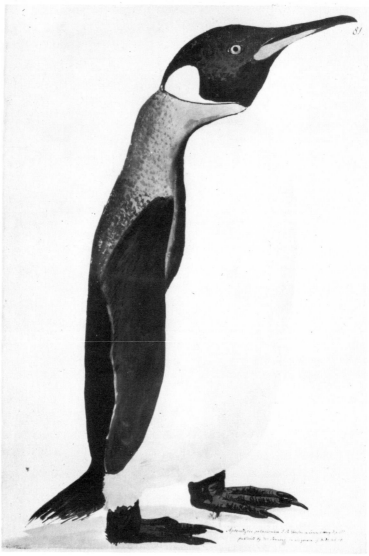

A penguin drawn by George Forster

Poetua, daughter of Omo, Chief of Raiatea, and one of the
hostages taken by Cook pending the finding of two deserters

Joshua Reynolds' portrait of Omai, who sailed from Tahiti in the *Adventure* and, backed by Banks, made a great impression on London society

and within two or three days they stretched from horizon to horizon. The temperature fell below freezing, and the forms of heating aboard the *Resolution* were so primitive that it was almost as cold inside the hull of the ship as it was on the upper deck. The elder Forster, in particular – in his defence it must be said that he was suffering very severely from rheumatism – complained bitterly about the conditions of his quarters, a cabin just abaft the mainmast, where sea-water and the Polar wind could, apparently, both enter at will. Forster rejoiced when they ran into foggy weather which, combined with the numerous icebergs in the vicinity, made for a very dangerous situation indeed and one that compelled Cook to turn northwards again.

He was given very little time to rejoice for a week before Christmas the weather cleared and Cook turned the *Resolution* south again. On the 21 December the *Resolution* crossed the Antarctic Circle, only the second time this had ever been done and both times by Cook. On Christmas Day they were still heading south and the elder Forster, in his journal for that day, did not know whether to be the most upset about his own sufferings, with the ice-bound Antarctic wastes which he compares unfavourably to hell, or with 'the execrations, oaths and curses' that assailed him on all sides as the crew of the *Resolution* celebrated their Christmas in the traditional naval manner.

For the time being, even Cook had had enough. He writes: 'Our ropes were like wires, sails like boards or plates of metal and the sheaves frozen fast in the blocks so that it required our utmost efforts to get a topsail up or down. The cold is so intense as hardly to be endured, the whole sea in a manner covered with ice, a hard gale and a thick fog. Under all these unfavourable circumstances,' he continues in a splendid under-statement, 'it was natural for me to think of returning more to the north'. So he turned north for the warmer latitudes of the forties, and probably not before time because George

Forster, the son of the elder, or complaining, Forster, says
that both health and morale aboard had reached a pretty low
state. His father and at least a dozen others were crippled and
unable to work because of rheumatics – although his father
was apparently not affected in his hands as the lamentations
continued to pour forth daily in his journal: when one considers that the entire interior of the *Resolution* was sodden and
dripping with damp and condensation it is surprising that
there were not more rheumatic casualties. There was, young
Forster went on, a general languor and sickly look among the
crew and even Captain Cook was pale and lean, having
entirely lost his appetite.

So northwards for fourteen days Captain Cook took them,
but he didn't remain north for very long. As soon as he was
convinced that his crew were fit again Cook, to the elder
Forster's unbelieving consternation and total horror, turned
the *Resolution* to the south again. When Cook had set his
face to a task he was not a man to turn lightly away from it: if
the southern continent was there, he was going to find it. He
didn't tell his officers and men what his destination was for
the excellent reason that he didn't know himself, but Forster,
in despair, was moved to write 'Nothing could be more de-
jecting than the entire ignorance of our future destination,
which, without apparent reason, was constantly kept a secret
to every person on the ship'.

For the third time, picking his way through the icebergs
and the ice-fields, Cook took the *Resolution* – surely there
was never a ship so aptly named – across the Antarctic Circle.
Cook's sheer icy courage marched well with the polar wastes
in which he now found himself. Few captains of today, with
powerfully engined and highly manoeuverable steel vessels,
would care to emulate what Cook did in that highly un-
maneouverable collier on that long ago January day in 1774,
where he was at the mercy of every vagary of wind and
current, beset by giant icebergs on every side and hardly able

to trim a sail, let alone raise or lower one, because of sails sheeted in ice until they were like iron, because of ropes that were no longer ropes but ice-sheathed, giant hawsers. But this is precisely what Cook did, nor did he stop short at the Antarctic Circle.

He kept on going south for another four days and then, on 30 January 1774 he stopped. He stopped because he had to because he had run up against a solid and impassable field of pack-ice that stretched from horizon to horizon. The latitude was 71° 10′ south, the longitude 106° 34′ west. This was the furthest south point that Cook reached, the furthest south point that any person had ever reached. It is worth noting in the passing that, from that day till the present time two hundred years later, no ship ever again has penetrated as far south in that region.

Cook, in his journal, intimates that he was not sorry that the decision as to whether he should push on even further to the south had been taken out of his hands. That same sentence in his diary, certainly the most quoted sentence Cook ever wrote, gives us the most revealing – indeed the only reveal- ing – statement that Cook ever made about himself and what drove him to embark upon that unparalleled series of explor- ations and discoveries. 'I who hope ambition leads me not only further than any other man has been before me, but as far as I think it possible for man to go, was not sorry at meeting with this interruption.'

Cook, it might be said, had rather cruel luck in not dis- covering Antarctica – and what a crowning triumph that would have been for a fabulous career. Even where he turned back, he was only about two hundred miles from the nearest coast. What has not been noted or remarked upon is that at Cook's furthest south position he was considerably further south – in some cases by over three hundred miles – than approximately half of the Antarctic coastline. Between ap- proximately longitude 170° east – which runs through the

South Island of New Zealand – and longitude 10° west – which lies roughly halfway between Cape Town and the east coast of South America – a rough semi-circle of the Antarctic coastline in the high latitudes of the Indian and Atlantic oceans lies between the Antarctic Circle and latitude 70° south. Cook, it will be remembered, had reached a latitude of more than 71° south. Had he attempted this, his deepest polar penetration, in the area above outlined he would certainly, given, of course, luck with the ice pack, have reached the coast of the Antarctic continent. As it happened, Cook made his effort in the high latitudes of the Pacific where the Antarctic coast-line recedes far to the south, in some areas at least seven hundred miles further south than in the Atlantic. But whether he discovered Antarctica or not, Cook's voyage in January 1774 still remains one of the most incredible that man has ever undertaken.

And so, having established beyond all question that Dalrymple's fabled continent existed in neither the Indian or Pacific oceans – there still existed the remote possibility that a very much reduced continent might be found in the high latitudes of the South Atlantic – Cook, to the unspeakable relief of the elder Forster, turned the *Resolution* north.

There arose now in Cook's mind the question as to what he should do next. He had accomplished, in the Indian and Pacific Oceans, virtually all he had set out to accomplish and was perfectly entitled to set out for home. The Horn was not all that far distant and he could be in the Atlantic in a few weeks. Or, if he so wished, he could refit and spend the winter in Cape Town and make another sortie into the polar regions the following summer. Neither of those courses appealed to Cook. When explorer's fever enters the blood-stream, there is only one way the ailment can progress – it becomes steadily worse and Cook's was now an incurable case. Except for a few uncertainly placed islands the whole of the South Pacific was still a vast unknown. What could be more obvious? What could be more suitable?

A man of Easter Island drawn by William Hodges

Cook summoned his officers and men – if he was going to
extend their voyage by another year the least he could do
would be to give them a chance to express their opinions –
and outlined his proposals to them. He had it in mind, he said,
to locate a land supposedly discovered by Juan Fernandez in
the eastern Pacific, then make for Easter Island. (Cook had no
great faith in his ability to find either. The authority for the

existence and position of the first was no less than Alexander Dalrymple and Cook's faith in Dalrymple was at its lowest ebb: Easter Island existed, no question about that, but, as Cook said, its situation was 'so variously laid down that I have little hope of finding it'.) From there he proposed to go clear across the Pacific to the west, almost as far as the coast of Australia, following a route that no explorer had done before. Then it was his intention to go to New Zealand, recross the Pacific, be round the Horn by November and then spend the summer exploring the high latitudes of the south Atlantic before making for Cape Town and home. Put briefly, it may not sound so much. In fact it was a monumental voyage which could not be accomplished in less than eighteen months.

There were no dissenting voices: everybody, it seems, was delighted at the prospect. This seems rather difficult to explain due to the fact that to the average Royal Navy seaman, then as now, the fairest sight on earth was the gangway that led from ship to shore. Perhaps they were so relieved to be escaping from the icy embrace of Antarctica that they would willingly and cheerfully have agreed to anything. More likely, many of them had been bitten by the explorer's bug themselves. Most likely, they were aware now that they were an elite, that they were achieving things that no men had ever achieved before and that they were in their own way making history: and those things were happening, they were well aware, because their almost idolised captain was making them happen. It is difficult to assess just what impact Cook's personality had on his crew but clearly it was somewhere in the range between 'great' and 'immense'. There was also, of course, the tremendous kudos attached to being on the *Resolution*: fifty years later, when some of the young men on board had become old, they had only to say 'I sailed with Captain Cook' and they were at once as men apart.

Juan Fernandez's land, to nobody's surprise, failed to

materialise: to Cook's mind, Dalrymple's authoritative assertion that it was there and in such and such a position was a positive guarantee that it didn't exist. On 23 February, Cook came to the conclusion that the land simply did not exist and laid off a course for where he thought Easter Island most likely to be.

It was at this point that Cook's health gave rise to the gravest anxiety. He had been through a tremendous physical and mental strain, he had spent most of his time in the Antarctic exposed to the bitter cold on deck, and the unhealthy diet hadn't helped. Now he had to take to bed with 'a bilious colic', he could retain neither food, drink nor medicines and his condition rapidly worsened from serious to critical. There seems to have been little doubt that he was suffering from an acute infection of the gall-bladder. There is no question that it was the surgeon's – Patten, by name – devoted and constant attention that saved Cook's life.

Cook was on deck again, but still convalescing, when Easter Island was raised on 12 March. The *Resolution* sailed along the coast looking for a harbour – there was none – the side of the ship lined with a crew that gazed in amazement at the massive stone statues that dotted the island, some on hillsides, some on massive stone platforms. When a party went ashore they were to find many more of those statues lying on their sides and almost overgrown by tall grass. The natives there, who proved quite friendly, had no idea who had built the statues or when. Cook's theory that the Polynesians were incapable of the art and mechanical engineering to carve and erect those giant statues and that they must have been the handiwork of an earlier and more advanced civilisation that has now vanished, is almost certainly correct: but the fact remains that the origin of the famous stone gods of Easter Island is still a complete mystery.

As a source of fresh provisions, Easter Island was a considerable disappointment. They couldn't even obtain fresh

Resolution Bay in the Marquesas based on a drawing by William Hodg

water there. Cook decided to sail to the Marquesas, which had been discovered by the Spanish almost two centuries previously: he wished to establish their position, which was only vaguely known: and he hoped to find fresh food supplies. En route to the Marquesas, Cook again became ill to the extent that his life was again despaired of. But once more, devoted nursing brought him through. The Marquesas, four high, razor-backed islands, were raised on 7 April and the *Resolution* anchored in Vaitahu Bay in the island of Tahuata the following day.

The islanders proved to be very friendly and although fresh meat was not obtainable there was plenty of fruit and some vegetables to be had. What struck the English most forcibly – and opinion aboard seems to have been unanimous on this point – was the appearance of the Marquesans themselves. A slim and graceful people, with skins so light that the women and children could easily be mistaken for Europeans, they were the most beautiful race of people that Cook and his men had ever seen, not just in the Pacific but in the world.

Cook now set sail for what had virtually become his second home – Tahiti. On the nine-day trip there they had to sail through the Tuamotu Archipelago, a far-scattered group of coral atolls. Cook attempted to land on one of those but the natives made it plain that they wanted no part of Cook or his men so he went on his way, anchoring in Matavai Bay in Tahiti on 22 April.

They received the now standard rapturous welcome. The island, which had hardly any pigs the last time Cook had visited it, now seemed to be positively over-run with them. Cook bought so many that he had to have a pig-sty built on shore. He was now running short of trading goods but discovered an excellent substitute currency in the form of quantities of red feathers they'd picked up the previous autumn in the Friendly Islands – Cook had until then been unaware that red was the colour sacred to the Tahitian god Oro and that red feathers, which appeared to be unobtainable in Tahiti itself, were regarded as being indispensable for the performance of certain religious ceremonies.

While they were there Cook and a party of officers and scientists were privileged to witness a most extraordinary spectacle in a nearby bay where the capital, Papeete, now stands. The Tahitians were preparing for an invasion of the neighbouring island of Moorea, whose chief was in revolt against Tahiti: this was the dress rehearsal. The bay was filled from end to end with a huge fleet of double-hulled war canoes, many almost as long as the *Resolution* itself. Those enormously high-powered vessels had a fighting platform aft on which stood the warriors armed with spears, clubs and a plentiful supply of stones. (It is an extraordinary thing that throughout the entire Polynesian Pacific – and nowhere else in the world – stones appeared to be the preferred offensive weapon.) Including the rowers, who would presumably also fight when the need arose, there were upwards of forty warriors in each canoe. And Cook counted no fewer than 160 such canoes: in addition he counted as many again of slightly smaller canoes which he took to be supply vessels and transports.

Some reports had it that several of the canoes were so large that they contained paddlers and warriors to a number close on two hundred, and this may well have been the case. In any event, it must have been a most impressive sight to see those hundreds of canoes and thousands of warriors lined up for revue.

Cook prudently didn't wait for the actual hostilities to commence. This time the leave-taking was especially painful for Cook told them sadly that he would never be returning to Tahiti. In point of fact he was back just over three years later.

From there they went to Huahine and Raiatea in the Society Group, islands almost as well known to them now as Tahiti

Some of Cook's men landing at Erromanga in the New Hebrides.
Several natives were killed and two of Cook's men were wounded

was. There they provisioned and there the broken-hearted
Odiddy was returned to his home. Thence they sailed west
towards the Friendly Islands, passing and naming Palmerston

Island, a coral atoll in the Cook Group. A few days later they
came to a much larger island where the air was so thick with
thrown spears and hurtling stones that it was impossible to
effect a landing. Savage Island, Cook called it, as well he
might, for had it not been for his own alacrity in moving to
one side he would have been transfixed by a spear. Descend-

ants of the stone-throwers maintain that their ancestors have been slandered and that the people of Niue – the original name and the one by which it is now known – are really as friendly as can be.

Cook moved on to the Friendly Islands which appeared to have the same fascination for him as did Tahiti. When he came back to these regions three years later he spent no less than three months cruising idly about these islands, seemingly unable to tear himself away. On this occasion, however, he did not delay. It was already the end of June, he wanted to round Cape Horn in November and before doing that he wished to investigate the existence of a group of islands that both Quiros and Bougainville claimed to exist about halfway between the Friendly Islands and the Australian coast.

From the Friendly – Tonga – Islands, Cook sailed the *Resolution* west by slightly north, just missing the Fiji Islands which lay slightly to the northward of his track. The first of the Great Cyclades, as Bougainville had named this group, an island called Maewo, was sighted on 17 July. From then on, Cook was to find himself continuously in a maze of islands – there are about eighty in all in the Great Cyclades, stretching over a distance of close on five hundred miles – chart-work in plenty for Cook to do.

They found that the Great Cyclades was the meeting place of two races, two cultures – the Polynesians and the darker-skinned and rather more negroid Melanesians. They exhibited a marked difference in temperament: uncompromising hostility to strangers appeared to be an ingrained character-istic of the Melanesian nature. When Cook effected a landing on two predominantly Melanesian Islands, Malekula and Erromanga, he was met with cold hostility which, in Erromanga, became very warm indeed when the natives tried to take possession of the *Resolution's* boats. Stones were thrown, spears were used and arrows were fired: the men of the *Resolution* had to have recourse to their muskets to save their lives. Several natives were killed and many injured: two English seamen were wounded.

For this, characteristically, Cook blamed only themselves. He wrote sadly: 'We enter their ports and attempt to land in a peaceable manner. If this succeeds, all is well, if not we land nevertheless and maintain our footing by the superiority of our firearms. In what other light can they first look upon us but as invaders of their country?' This is a recurrent theme in Cook's journals. Unlike the great majority of his fellow countrymen – come to that, fellow Europeans – he was very conscious of and sensitive to the fact that they were forcing their unwanted attentions upon people who had been perfectly happy before they came along, that they, the white men, were taking by force that which rightfully belonged to others and that in the long run the advent of the white men could only bring decay and destruction to those simple and once contented Pacific peoples – this thought does appear to have genuinely haunted Cook: paradoxically – or so it would seem – when it came to speed in annexing new territories for the crown there was no one in the exploring business who could hold a candle to Cook. But, of course, it was really no paradox, just the age-old struggle between duty and conscience.

The Polynesian element in the Great Cyclades gave Cook a rather different reception. He was badly in need of water and wood so he tried his luck at the most southerly of the major islands in the group, Tanna, the site of a still active volcano. The people there were Polynesian and although the original reception was cool, a very close friendship eventually developed, despite the fact that one of the natives was shot by a sentry for no apparent reason. If the trail of natives left dead in a large variety of Pacific islands be taken as any criterion, the marines aboard Cook's ships appear to have been a very trigger-happy lot indeed.

The islanders of Tanna were more than eager to trade and

A woman from the Island of Tanna drawn by William Hodges

Cook was able to stock up to his satisfaction in fresh meat –
the inevitable pigs. When Cook left after what was one of his
most enjoyable and pleasant stays in the Pacific – for friendliness, Cook classed them with the Tahitians and the natives
of the Friendly Islands – he had two observations to make: he
regarded Tanna as the most fertile island in the Pacific, a

A man from Tanna drawn by William Hodges

circumstance he attributed to the volcanic ash which was deposited at regular intervals over the island; he further regarded it as the most beautiful place he had ever seen. Coming from a confirmed Tahitian like Cook, this was compliment indeed.

Cook headed north to make another sweep through the

Great Cyclades to complete his surveying and chart-work, then turned south for New Zealand. In Cook's opinion Bougainville, the French explorer, had barely touched upon this group of islands whereas he, Cook, had visited all the major and many of the minor islands and had thoroughly surveyed and charted the whole, not forgetting to bestow names freely as he passed along. Cook, accordingly, thought he had a better right to it than Bougainville, re-christened it the New Hebrides and annexed it in the name of the crown. It worked – it still is predominantly British, part of an Anglo-French condominion.

They sailed steadily south till on 5 September they saw a mountainous island rising out of the sea. To the north were a series of very dangerous reefs and shoals so Cook cruised down the east coast till he found a suitable anchorage. The natives of the islands – an unknown race to Cook, not Polynesians – proved to be very hospitable and the *Resolution* stayed there for a week. In a land that Cook found very like Australia the inhabitants, a friendly people much given to laughter, carried on a fairly intensive form of cultivation.

During his stay Cook climbed a mountain and discovered that the island, in the shape of an enormous whale-back, was about thirty-five miles wide. When they went on their way again they were astonished at its north-south length, which was at least two hundred and fifty miles. Cook reckoned that, New Zealand apart, it must be the biggest island in the Pacific and, as usual, Cook was right. Apparently not caring for its native name of Balade, Cook changed it to New Caledonia.

On 10 October they came across a small, uninhabited but fertile island which Cook called Norfolk Island. He stopped off just long enough to annex it then carried on by the way of the west coast of North Island to Queen Charlotte Sound, where he arrived on 18 October.

Three weeks were spent there, laying in water and wood and getting the *Resolution* in the best possible condition before setting off on the next long leg of their journey – round Cape Horn and on to Cape Town which would be the first place where they could hope to obtain provisions. From tree-stumps that showed that a saw had been used, Cook knew that another vessel had been there. The message he'd left for Furneaux was gone. And, by using sign language and diagrammatic sketches with the Maoris, Cook was able to establish roughly the date when the *Adventure* had left.

Cook noted that the Maoris had changed since he had last been there, just under a year previously. Then they had been friendly, gregarious: now they were withdrawn, shy, wary. It was not until Cook arrived in Cape Town and found there a letter left for him by Furneaux and learned of the cannibal episode that he understood that the Maoris of Queen Charlotte Sound had indeed something to be wary of.

The *Resolution* left the Sound on 10 November, steered on a south-east course till she was about a thousand miles south of her starting point, then turned east, making a very fast passage to Cape Horn, the powerful westerlies behind her, more or less along the 55th parallel. Furneaux had gone almost exactly the same way: neither of them, it need hardly be said, encountered any trace of Dalrymple's continent.

The trip to Cape Horn was uneventful. Cook even says it was boring. They spent the Christmas period in the Tierra del Fuego region, surveying, botanising, taking on food and water and then rounded the Horn on 29 December, moving out into the Atlantic.

Cook's last objective now was to cross the South Atlantic in the high latitudes in what he was convinced would be the vain task of locating the land – part of the great continent of the south – which Dalrymple and other illustrious geographers maintained to be there: as far as they were concerned it had to be, they'd already drawn maps of it.

So Cook moved deep into the regions of ice and bitter cold and dense blanketing fogs again. He discovered South Georgia, a bleak and barren and desolate wilderness of ice and snow, uninhabited, and totally useless for any purpose: this, of course, did not prevent Cook from going ashore and annexing it in the name of the crown. Further on he discovered an equally useless group of isles which he annexed and called the South Sandwich Islands, and, to the south of that, another desolation which he called Southern Thule.

Those apart, Cook hunted high and he hunted low, but never a trace of this land of Dalrymple, far less the great Southern Continent did he see for the reason that had been obvious to Cook for a long time now – it just wasn't there to be seen. For a final week or two Cook searched again for Bouvet's Cape Circumcision and failed to find it. He now intersected the track he had made over two years ago when he first crossed the Antarctic Circle. He had circumnavigated the world in latitudes so high that such a voyage had been regarded as quite impossible; and he had put the final nails in the coffin of Dalrymple's dream, having proved, not only beyond reasonable doubt, but absolutely, that no such thing as a Southern Continent existed. Cook had been given a job, or if you like, he'd given himself a job to do and he'd done it.

It was time to go home now, if for no other reason than that there didn't seem to be anything left for him in the southern hemisphere to explore. He reached Cape Town on 21 March where a number of repairs, chiefly to a badly damaged rudder, kept him for five weeks. It was here that he was given the letter left him by Furneaux and learnt of the tragedy that had taken place in Queen Charlotte Sound.

The *Resolution's* homeward route was by St Helena, Ascension Island, and the Azores. She anchored at Spithead on 30 July 1775, three years and eighteen days after setting out on what was to be, and what still remains, as the greatest voyage of exploration in history.

CHAPTER 6

THE NORTH-WEST
PASSAGE

At the end of this second voyage there was no doubt at all,
as there had been at the end of the first one, to whom all
the honour and credit belonged. Cook was the man of the
hour and, in a strangely quiet way, a national hero. He was
made a Fellow of the Royal Society. He was given the
Copley Gold Medal for his paper on the advancement of
health at sea (his stringent enforcement of the rules for
combating scurvy is not actually mentioned). In all of that
incredible voyage Cook had lost only one man, and that not
through scurvy. He was an intimate of the Lords of the
Admiralty. He was received by the king, promoted to post-
captain in command of *H.M.S. Kent*, a seventy-four gun
cruiser, then made captain at Greenwich Hospital which was
the Admiralty's way of saying that, even at the age of forty-
seven, he had done more than enough and was entitled to
honourable – and full-paid – retirement.

Cook himself wasn't so sure about this sinecure. To a
friend he wrote: 'My fate drives me from one extreme to
another. A few months ago the whole southern hemisphere
was hardly big enough for me, and now I am going to be
confined within the limits of Greenwich Hospital, which
are far too small for an active mind like mine. I must confess
it is a fine retreat and a pretty income, but whether I can
bring myself to like ease and retirement time will show'.

Cook was needlessly concerned. His time for ease and
retirement was not yet come, tragically it was never to come.

Plans were already afoot for a third great voyage but not, this time, to the South Seas. While Cook was busily engaged in writing up, for publication, the journal of his second voyage – having read the botch Hawkesworth had made of his previous journal he was determined to supervise this one himself – the Admiralty were considering the possibility, advisability and wisdom of trying to force the fabled North-West Passage, a dream that had been in the minds of men for close on three centuries. The idea was, simply, that between the Atlantic and the Pacific there might exist a passage around the top of North America. Many attempts, attempts associated with names like Cabot and Frobisher and Hudson and Baffin, had been made over the years. Baffin, at the end of the previous century, had actually reached the astonishing latitude of $77° 45'$ north – almost halfway between the Arctic Circle and the Pole, an achievement that still stood a hundred years after the time of Cook. But even he had failed to find the North-West Passage.

The Admiralty was determined to try once more. This time, however, it was intended to make a double-pronged attack. It was known that in 1742 Bering, a Swede serving in the Russian Navy, had established that a strait existed between the Asiatic mainland and the north-west tip of North America which we now call Alaska. A simultaneous attack, it was decided, would be made on the Passage, one expedition approaching from the Atlantic side while a second would approach from the Pacific side.

The Atlantic approach would be made by the frigate *Lion*, commanded by Cook's old friend Richard Pickersgill, while the Pacific end would be attempted by the *Resolution* and the *Discovery* – not the original *Discovery*, which was not available, but a new one, another Whitby collier which the Admiralty acquired on Cook's recommendation.

The question arose in the minds of the Admiralty as to who should command the Pacific expedition. Cook, of

John Montagu, Fourth Earl of Sandwich, by Thomas Gainsborough

course, was the blindingly obvious choice, not just the best man but the only man, but the Admiralty, having regard to Cook's massive achievements and the fact that they'd given him a richly-earned retirement, were markedly reluctant to approach him. Instead they hit upon what they probably regarded as the extremely ingenious and cunning plan of asking him along to a very exclusive dinner party where the other three guests were Lord Sandwich, First Lord of the Admiralty, Palliser, Comptroller of the Navy, and Stephens, Secretary to the Admiralty, and, once having got him there, of asking his advice as the man best fitted to command the Pacific expedition. It is perhaps superfluous to add that when Cook left the table he did so as commander of the expedition.

As his first lieutenant, Cook had John Gore, who had been round the world with Cook in the *Endeavour* and with Wallis in the *Dolphin*, James King – also an accomplished astronomer – as second officer and a John Williamson as third. The master was a man who was to become almost as famous as Cook himself – William Bligh.

The *Discovery* was commanded by Captain James Clerke, a close friend of Cook and one of the most experienced seamen of the time – he'd been round the world with Byron and twice round the world with Cook so that he was now embarking upon his fourth great voyage. It was also to be his final voyage. Like Cook, he was to leave his bones on the shores of the Pacific. His first lieutenant was a James Burney, his second a John Rickman. Among his midshipmen was a George Vancouver (who had also sailed with Cook in the *Resolution*) who was to become a noted explorer in his own right. Over twenty members of the expedition had already sailed with Cook, some of them twice. Among the latter was Samuel Gibson of the Marines (now a sergeant) whom Cook had had flogged for deserting the ship and taking to the hills with a native girl on their first visit to Tahiti. Clearly, Gibson was no man to bear grudges. And with them was to go Omai, a Tahitian whom Furneaux had brought back to England.

On 12 July 1776, four years but a day from the time he had sailed on his previous voyage, Captain Cook sailed again for the Pacific. He had to sail alone, for the unfortunate Captain Clerke of the *Discovery* was at the time languishing in a debtor's gaol – he had guaranteed the debts of his brother Captain John Clerke who had departed for foreign parts without settling them. He was finally released and the *Discovery* set sail on 1 August – hardly the most auspicious beginning for a voyage. It is believed that it was while he was in prison that Clerke contracted the tuberculosis that was eventually to kill him.

On the way to Cape Town the *Resolution* stopped at Tenerife to take aboard the usual copious quantities of wine and to top up her water supplies. Here, too, she took aboard most unusual provisions – animal fodder, for the *Resolution* was a veritable floating farmyard well-stocked with cattle and pigs and sheep and goats, all personal presents from the king to be given to various islands in the Pacific – although taking pigs to the Pacific, which teemed with them, does seem rather like carrying coals to Newcastle.

Cape Town was reached on 17 October. Cook immediately had ship-fitters busy re-caulking the *Resolution*, which had leaked so abominably, especially through the main deck, on the way down that there was scarce a man, Cook wrote, who could lie dry in his bed. When the *Discovery* arrived on 10 November she was found to be in as bad a condition as the *Resolution*: she, too, was immediately in the shipwrights' hands.

Cook had put the stock ashore to graze and when some of the sheep were stolen he had them replaced with Cape sheep and, clearly considering that his menagerie was not yet complete, he brought aboard rabbits and no fewer than four horses which he stabled in Omai's cabin, which Omai ap-

A painting by Webber of Cook meeting some Maoris at a settlement in Queen Charlotte Sound in February 1777; *Resolution* and *Discovery* can be seen in the background

parently accepted with much willingness, for Cook, in his
last ever letter to Lord Sandwich, dated 26 November 1776,
wrote: 'The taking on board of some horses has made Omai

completely happy, he consented with raptures to give up his cabin to make room for them'. Still speaking of the livestock, Cook went on in one of his rare lighter moments: 'Nothing is wanting but a few females of our own species to make the *Resolution* a complete ark'. It was in this same letter that Cook said, almost as if he were composing an epitaph for himself: 'My endeavour shall not be wanting to accomplish the great object of this voyage'. Endeavour and achievement: those were the corner-stones of Cook's life.

The two ships sailed in company on the first day of December. On the 13th he located and named a group of islands the Prince Edward Group – they had, in fact, first been seen by the Frenchman Marion du Fresne, but Cook was not going to let a trifle like that prevent him from re-christening them and annexing them for the crown. (They now belong to South Africa.) Twelve days later Cook found Kerguelen Island which had eluded him in his search for it some four years' previously. The first island had been named by Kerguelen – Isle of Rendezvous. Cook promptly changed it to Bligh's Cap, after his master, remarking that none but seabirds would ever rendezvous in that barren, treeless, desolate island.

Driven along by the strong westerlies, the two vessels made excellent time and reached Van Diemen's Land – Tasmania – on 26 January. Here they watered and took on wood and struck up some sort of acquaintanceship with the very backward aborigines who lived there – their women, Samwell, the surgeon, wrote, were the ugliest creatures that can be imagined in human shape, and if the drawings made of them by Webber, the *Resolution's* official artist, are in any way representational one has to admit that it is difficult to fault Samwell's judgment.

The two ships sailed on the 30 January, and on 12 February arrived in New Zealand at that anchorage that was now as familiar to Cook as Matavai Bay in Tahiti – Queen Charlotte

Sound. He found the Maoris there in a very apprehensive state indeed: they assumed – by their code it was inevitable – that Cook had come to take revenge for the death of the ten men from Furneaux' *Discovery*. They could not understand Cook's 'Let bygones be bygones' attitude and were dumbfounded when Cook, having discovered the identity of the man who had instigated the slaughter – their chief, Kahura – did not have him dispatched on the spot. Cook refused. He wrote: 'If I had followed the advice of our pretended friends I might have extirpated the whole race, for all the people of each hamlet, or village, by turns, applied to me to destroy the others, a most striking proof of the divided state in which they live'. Instead of having him executed, Cook had his portrait painted by Webber. A classic example, indeed, of turning the other cheek: unfortunately we do not know whether this gesture had any mollifying effect on Kahura's bloodthirsty nature.

After a fortnight the two ships left for Tahiti. It had been Cook's intention to proceed there by the most direct course but easterly headwinds slowed him up and kept on bearing him westwards off his course. Land was first sighted on 29 March – Mangaia, one of the islands in the Cook Group. The combination of the fierce surf and coral reefs that surrounded the island made it impossible to bring off provisions. They tried another island in the same group with the same results.

The obtaining of fresh fodder for the livestock had now became a matter of urgency. Rather than fight his way to Tahiti against the easterlies, which might have taken weeks, Cook decided to run west to the Friendly Islands where he knew he would be welcomed and where he knew that fodder in plenty could be had. En route they stopped off at the uninhabited Palmerston Island, which Cook had discovered on his previous voyage, and obtained some scurvy grass there.

The *Resolution* arrived in the Friendly Islands late in April and was to remain there – with the *Discovery* – until mid-

A reception staged for Cook on an island of the Ha'apai Group

July. This period in Cook's life has given rise to considerable speculation among historians. Why, they have asked, did he not strike out for the North Pacific and try to force the Bering Strait that summer – even though it might have been rather late in the summer before he got there. The answer to that is straightforward: the Admiralty's plan was that the attack on the North-West Passage was to be a co-ordinated one from the Atlantic and the Pacific, in the hope that the two expeditions might meet, and the date fixed for the attempt was 1778 – the following summer. The Admiralty had taken into account the possibility that Cook could well have been delayed on the outward voyage and so might have failed to make the rendezvous in the summer of 1777. In fact, Cook had made a very fast passage out and could have reached the Bering Strait that summer had he tried. But that would have been pointless: 1778 was the fixed date.

What is puzzling about this period is that Cook, that driving restless man with the insatiable urge to see what lay over the hill, round the next corner, appeared, temporarily at least, to have lost all his old zest for exploring. He was told not once but many times of the existence of the Samoan Islands to the north and the Fiji Islands to the north-west, both of which were, in terms of Cook's previous far-reaching sweeps across the Pacific, virtually on the door-step of the Friendly Islands. And he was told about dozens of other islands at not too great a distance from Tongatabu. Cook let them all lie and continued this seemingly aimless wandering among the enchanted isles of the Tongas. So easy-going and relaxed had Cook become that girls from the Friendly Islands lived aboard ship and drifted with them from island to island in this dream-like idyllic period.

Like a soccer player or cricketer who has played too much, perhaps Cook had for the moment gone stale, the results of his massive labours over the years having at last caught up with

Webber's drawing of natives of Tonga boxing

An engraving, after a drawing by Webber, of a 'night dance' by
men from the Ha'apai Group of islands

him. Perhaps he was deliberately relaxing himself and his
crews so that they should all be in the peak of condition when

160

they made their assault on the Bering Strait. Perhaps it was
just because he loved the Friendly Islands, which he did. Or
perhaps he had the premonition that, for him, now was all
the time there was going to be and he was making the most

161

of it. We shall never know: Cook, inevitably, makes no mention in his journal of the reason for his delay.

On 17 July, the two vessels set out for Tahiti where they arrived on 12 August. Here again Cook was to display the same puzzling inactivity, pleasantly whiling away his time with his by now old and trusted friends in Tahiti and the neighbouring Society Islands. The livestock were disembarked at Matavai Bay and Cook writes with amusement in his journal of the sensation caused among the Tahitians when he and Captain Clerke cantered across the plain on their horses, animals that the Tahitians had never seen before.

It is, parenthetically, a matter for wonder that Clerke was able to ride a horse at all. The first signs of his consumption – tuberculosis – had appeared shortly after leaving England and the disease was now in a fairly advanced condition: although tuberculosis is readily curable today, at that time the progress of the disease was irreversible. Frequently he was so ill that he was unfit to command the *Discovery*. Indeed, so much had his health failed that is was suggested that he remain behind in Tahiti while Burney, his first lieutenant, took the *Discovery* north: but Clerke insisted on going.

Cook does seem to have become increasingly autocratic in his dealing with the islanders. When they left Tahiti they went first to Moorea, only a dozen miles away. A goat was stolen and Cook let it be known if it were not returned forthwith he would destroy every canoe on the island, a measure that would have had a crippling effect on the island's food supplies and economy – a rather extreme measure, one would have thought, to take to ensure the return of one goat. In point of fact, a dozen canoes were burnt before the goat was returned.

Again, in Huahine, a sextant was stolen. The sextant was recovered and the thief apprehended. The thief was so unrepentant and insolent that Cook had his ears cut off – again, one would have thought, a punishment that somewhat

A portrait of John Webber, the official artist on Cook's final voyage and the painter of the 'death scene' on the jacket. This portrait is from a miniature by J. D. Mottet

A sextant made by Jesse Ramsden, who also made sextants for Cook

exceeded the crime. In the next island they visited, Raiatea, Cook reverted to his common practice of seizing hostages. Two of his men deserted and Cook at once took prisoner the son, son-in-law and daughter of the chief of the island, a man who had always treated him with the greatest kindness and hospitality. The hostages were released when the deserters were returned. It is worth noting that Cook's tactics roused the islanders to such a fury of resentment that they actually tried to kidnap Cook and Clerke. In retrospect – in hindsight wisdom comes easily – Cook should have taken warning from this but clearly he didn't. Unquestionably, this policy of taking hostages worked. To us, today, it may seem a rather harsh policy and one difficult to condone, but then it has to be remembered that Cook was an eighteenth-century man dealing with a Polynesian mentality of that time that is totally alien to us. Cook was a highly intelligent man, he was the man on the spot and we cannot doubt that he knew exactly what he was doing. Besides, it is difficult to see what else he could have done.

The two vessels sailed on 7 December. On the 22nd they crossed the equator and on the 24th they discovered a bleak and uninhabited island which Cook called Christmas Island. Cook decided to stay there for a few days – he stayed for nine – partly because fish and turtle abounded, partly to give the crews a break over the Christmas period – after having spent seven months doing nothing except virtually loaf around the Pacific one would hardly have thought that they required one.

While they were there Cook, his second officer King, and Bayly the astronomer, went ashore to observe an eclipse of the sun to enable them to establish their exact longitude and also check on the accuracy of the chronometers. It is significant that Clerke did not accompany them: he was too ill to do so.

The vessels continued on their way and on 18 January two mountainous islands were sighted. Cook had made his last major discovery – the Hawaiian Islands. The two islands, Niihau and Kauai, were the two westernmost of the major islands in the Hawaiian group. Cook called them the Sandwich Isles – the name of his friend, patron and First Lord, the Earl of Sandwich, is scattered far and wide across the Pacific and the Atlantic – but they are now known as the Hawaiian Islands. The major island of the group, and the most easterly, Cook did not discover until later in the year. This was the island that was to give the group its name, Hawaii itself.

After what was now almost the standard opening gambit of shooting and killing a native without provocation, Cook

A portable observatory designed by William Bayly,

established an excellent relationship with the Hawaiians. They appeared to regard him as some sort of God for as soon as he stepped on the beach they fell prostrate and remained so until Cook signalled them to rise.

Cook found them a very attractive people. They were friendly, hospitable, did not bear arms and, compared to the average run of Polynesians, extremely honest. They pointed out to Cook another island standing to the west which they called Oahu. Cook felt he could not afford the time to explore it. It was a pity for then he would certainly have found the magnificent Pearl Harbour, where the Japanese naval air forces destroyed the United States Pacific fleet in December 1941. There too, today, stands Honolulu, the capital of the Hawaiian group.

On 2 February the ships headed north-east for New Albion – the west coast of North America – which they reached on

6 March between the 44th and 45th parallel – near a promontory named by Cook as Cape Foul Weather (the name has remained) in view of the extremely unpleasant weather that was to occur immediately afterwards. During the next month the ships were to encounter a succession of extremely unpleasant gales which made their northwards progress very slow. Unfavourable winds made it advisable to stand well off

A Sandwich Islander

Resolution and *Discovery* in Nootka Sound where the *Resolution* underwent some major repairs

the coast with the result that they missed both the mouth of the Columbia River and Juan de Fuca Strait, which leads up to the site of the present city of Vancouver.

Both ships had been so severely battered since leaving Cape Foul Weather that repairs were urgent and they were fortunate enough to find a sheltered inlet called Nootka Sound which Cook assumed to be on the mainland. In fact, it is about two-thirds of the way up the west coast of Vancouver Island. This was on 30 March. There they stayed for close

on four weeks – a tree had to be cut down to make a new mizzen mast for the *Resolution* – while Cook made the acquaintance of the natives, who, with their broad flat faces and high cheekbones were clearly not Polynesians – they were probably of Eskimo stock. They were a friendly, mild, inoffensive people which one might judge from the fact that on this occasion it wasn't found necessary to shoot any of them.

In sea-going condition again, the ships moved out on 26 April and turned north. The waters here are difficult and treacherous to a degree, calling for navigation of the highest order. Cook was back at the top of his form, surveying, charting and naming everything he could see, although clearly even his seemingly endless inventiveness was running out for he was beginning to repeat himself with names already used in the South Seas.

The coast-line had been steadily tending to the west and now it ran due west – the ships were running along the southern shores of Alaska. The *Resolution* was now leaking so badly that Cook was compelled to find some sheltered anchorage which he did in an inlet now known as Prince William Sound. She was careened and it was found that the seams between the timbers were wide open with hardly a trace of oakum left.

Repairs effected, they moved to the south-west round a very long promontory now known as the Kenai Peninsula. To the west of this peninsula a wide inlet stretched away to the north-east and some of the officers suggested that this might indeed be the entrance to the south-west passage. Cook had his reservations, but agreed to try it. For two hundred long miles they sailed up this inlet and not until its very end, with snow and ice covered mountains to right and left and dead ahead, did they know that what they had sailed up was a land-locked fjord.

Back at sea again, they sailed down the three hundred mile length of the Alaskan Peninsula and then its broken-up continuation, the Aleutian Islands. They paused briefly at one of those islands, Unalaska, sailed north-east up the far side of the Alaskan Peninsula, then north-east and north into Norton Sound. It was during this passage that the chief surgeon, Anderson, died of tuberculosis: it had been proposed that he, like Captain Clerke, should have been left behind in Tahiti. It would probably have made no difference: they would have died anyway.

At the northern end of Norton Sound lies a promontory which Cook named Cape Prince of Wales, the most westerly point of all the Americas and the nearest point to the Asiatic mainland. It was to this Asiatic mainland that Cook now sailed across the Bering Strait, anchoring in a sheltered inlet that he called the Bay of St Lawrence, paying a nice compliment to Bering who, just half a century earlier, had given the name of St. Lawrence to an island just south of the Bering Strait. The natives there he found to be courteous if withdrawn and, judging by both their behaviour and their substantial housing, quite the most advanced race he had encountered anywhere in the Pacific.

From the Bay of St Lawrence, the *Resolution* and the *Discovery* moved north through the Bering Strait, crossed the Arctic Circle then moved out into the Chukchi Sea, an arm of the Arctic Ocean. They did not move very far. Within three days – between 14 and 17 August, the temperature had fallen dramatically, the weather had sharply deteriorated and suddenly they found themselves up against an apparently solid wall of pack-ice that stretched from horizon to horizon. For a week Cook cast about with his usual determination to try to find some lead through the ice. He tried to break out by running along the northern shore of Siberia but again he was stopped by solid pack ice. The summer was almost over, if they lingered too long they might be trapped in the ice and remain there indefinitely: Cook decided to go south, winter in the Sandwich Islands (the Hawaiian Group) and try again the following summer. Indolent Cook may have appeared in the South Seas the previous year, but when there was a definite goal to be achieved he would achieve it, if it were possible for any man to do so: as he had said to Lord Sandwich, his endeavour would not be wanting to achieve the great object of the voyage.

They re-passed the Circle and the Bering Strait and went south to Unalaska in the Aleutians where Cook deemed it prudent to put in on 2 October: the *Resolution* was suffering

Cook meets the Chukchi at St Lawrence Bay, Siberia, on 10
August 1778

from her old troubles again, water coming in as through a
sieve in the uncaulked seams between her timbers. During
their three week stay there, Cook met Russian traders who
obligingly filled in missing portions of his charts or pointed
out existing errors in the charts he had been given: during
this time, also, he got to know the Eskimos fairly well, the
most peaceable and inoffensive people he reported he had
ever met.

The ships left for the Sandwich Islands on 24 October reaching them on 26 November, a voyage uneventful except for a severe gale in which the *Discovery's* main tack broke, killing one man and injuring several others. They sighted the island of Maui, the second most easterly and the second largest in the group. The two ships lay to off-shore – there seemed to be no suitable anchorages – and many natives came out in their canoes carrying quantities of more than welcome fresh fruit, vegetables and, of course, the inevitable pigs. Among those who came out was a venerable old gentleman who, from the very considerable respect accorded him by the others, appeared to be someone of considerable importance: he was, in fact, the King of Hawaii.

They moved on from Maui and a day or two later the towering, snow-topped twin peaks of Hawaii Island came into sight: both are about 13,700 feet. Cook moved slowly round the coast looking for a suitable harbour. Everywhere they went they were accompanied by large numbers of canoes, the occupants of which came aboard the ships with a total lack of fear that Cook had not experienced before in the Pacific. Their canoes, Cook noted without comment, were laden with hogs and women, the latter more willing to bestow their favours than any before encountered. Certain it is that the Hawaiians were a trusting lot. They cheerfully slept on deck at night while their canoes were towed behind the ships. Because of adverse winds it took the ships a long time to beat round the south coast of the island and start moving up the west coast. Not until 16 January was a likely anchorage seen in Kealakekua Bay. William Bligh was sent ashore to investigate and returned to pronounce the bay admirable for their purposes. There was a plentiful supply of water and two villages, Kekua and Kavarua, which would doubtless supply all their wants.

The reception awaiting Cook and his men when they anchored their ships in Kealakekua Bay the following morning, cannot possibly, it seems certain, have had any precedent in the history of the Pacific. King, Cook's second lieutenant, estimated that no fewer than one thousand five hundred canoes carrying at least nine thousand natives came out to meet them, hundreds more came out on surfboards, still hundreds more swam around like shoals of fish while thousands lined the shores of the bay.

Palea, a chief, and Koa, a high priest, came aboard and treated Cook with a deference amounting to reverence and when Cook was ceremoniously escorted ashore the waiting thousands prostrated themselves on the beach. Afterwards he was forced to sit through a long and peculiar ceremony, either of welcome or of initiation, in any event one with obviously religious overtones, before being allowed back to the ship. Cook did not know it, but he was being deified. Hawaiian folk-lore had it that one of their gods, Lono, the god of happiness and peace and agriculture, had sailed away over the sea long aeons ago, but was some day to return to them. Cook was Lono come home again and the *Resolution* was his temple. News of his coming had spread through the Hawaiian Islands since he had landed in Niihau and Kauai just a year previously, and, of course, he had been sighted off the coast of the island of Hawaii itself weeks before he had reached his final anchorage. This, of course, explained why, although there were only two small villages ashore, tens of thousands had waited to welcome him. They had had plenty of warning and they had come from afar to welcome their god home.

Cook does not appear to have been overly impressed by his deification. He was much happier just to have discovered Hawaii, as any explorer would have been. He writes: 'few . . . now lamented our having failed in our endeavour to find a northern passage homeward last summer. To this disappointment we owed our having it in our power to revisit the Sandwich Isles, and to enrich our voyage with a discovery which, though the last, seemed, in every respect, to be the most important that had hitherto been made by Europeans throughout the extent of the Pacific Ocean'. These are the very last words that Cook ever wrote in his journal. It is pleasant indeed that it should end on so gratified and contented a note.

An observatory and tents were put up on shore near the village of Kekua, which was the watering place. The ships were brought in close just in case – and it seemed a most unlikely event – that covering fire would ever be required

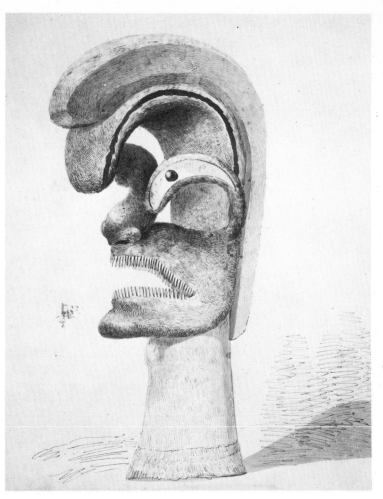

A basket-work figure of a Hawaiian god drawn by Webber

for naval personnel ashore. Kekua lay to the east of the bay. To the north-west lay the village of Kavarua, the place where Cook usually landed and where the king, Kalaniopu, lived while he was in residence.

He was not, in fact, in residence at the time, but he turned up on 24 January and proved to be the same venerable old

John Webber's painting of Tahitians dancing

George Carter's version of the death of Captain Cook in 1779

An early nineteenth-century Rockingham figure of Cook based on the portrait (facing p. 56) by Nathaniel Dance

gentleman who had boarded the *Resolution* at Maui. He came aboard the *Resolution* on a private visit, accompanied only by his immediate family: the following day, with great pomp and circumstance, a state visit was made, the king magnificently attired and attended by all his court retinue. Valuable presents were exchanged, King Kalaniopu gave Cook half-a-dozen extremely valuable feather cloaks while Cook went to the extent of giving the king his own belt and sword, and names were exchanged, this, in the Pacific of that time, being an indication of friendship for eternity. Everything seemed set fair.

But the barometer read wrong and eternity was to last only a very short time indeed. Within a week the entire demeanour of the people had changed. They began to make it unmistakably known that they thought it high time that their God was on his way again. They pointed out to the sailors how well and fit they were now looking and that there seemed to be no reason for their staying any longer. It has been suggested that the hosts were becoming tired of guests that were so very expensive to keep, and that the crews of two ships did consume a lot of food. Now, this is very true and was possibly a considerable factor in the change of attitude: on the other hand they – the English – had been there only a fortnight and had stayed for many times longer than that in various parts of the Pacific without wearing out their welcome: and Cook had always been scrupulous in paying for any provisions he obtained.

What is very possible is that the priests felt that, with a returned god among them, they had been deprived of both their spiritual and temporal powers, that their authority, which they cherished highly, had been diminished and if the people lost their habit of respect for them, they, the priests, would find it increasingly difficult to regain it with the passing of time. They may well have put this same argument to the king in respect of himself and as the king was an old worn-out man long past his best both physically and mentally, he may well have agreed with their point of view and given at least his tacit consent to propagandising among the people the advisability of Cook's early departure.

However it may have been, Cook was a man who could always take a hint. He had the observatory and the tents dismantled and brought aboard. King Kalaniopu appeared and presented him with most expensive gifts, whether as a token of genuine esteem or to speed the parting guest we cannot tell. Cook's plan now was to complete the surveying of the Hawaiian Islands and then move up to Kamchatka on the east coast of Asia before making his second attempt on the North-West Passage. They left on 4 February, to what appeared to be a genuinely affectionate farewell from a huge crowd. It is not impossible that a major factor of the apparent affection was their relief in seeing the guests depart.

When Cook returned only six days later, the affection was much less in evidence. It was clear that nobody from Kalaniopu down welcomed the return of the two ships. But Cook had had little option: in a severe gale two days previously the foremast of the *Resolution* had suffered such severe damage that it was essential to have it unstepped and repaired.

Relations became quickly very strained then developed into open hostility. A native who had been caught in the act of theft received forty lashes. Other natives who had been helping a naval watering party were driven off by their priests. For the first time the natives started carrying arms and became insolent and mocking in their behaviour. When a thief made off with some armourer's tools in a canoe and escaped on shore, Edgar, the master of the *Discovery* went ashore with some others and tried to confiscate the canoe. A fight broke out, the Hawaiians resorted to the inevitable stones and Edgar and his men were forced to abandon the pinnace they had come ashore in and swim out to the harbour for safety. What made matters worse was that the canoe – it had been stolen – was the property of a chief who had not only been very friendly but of the greatest assistance to Cook.

Cook was furious when he heared the news. King reported that Cook said: 'I am afraid that these people will oblige me to use some violent measures: for they must not be left to imagaine that they have gained an advantage over us'.

Alas for Cook, the opportunity to use those violent measures arose early the next morning, 14 February 1779. Clerke reported to Cook that his large cutter had been stolen during the night. Cook didn't hesitate. He at once set about the hostage tactic that had served him so well in the past. Kalaniopu would be brought aboard the *Resolution* and held there until the cutter and the armourer's tools were returned.

Cook went ashore with armed marines in a cutter, pinnace and launch and landed at Kavarua. The three boats moved some little distance off-shore while Cook and ten armed marines – including their commanding officer, Lieutenant Molesworth Phillips – marched to King Kalaniopu's house and insisted that he come immediately aboard the *Resolution*. The old king raised no objections but as they neared the water's edge one of his elderly wives ran up and weepingly begged him not to go aboard, a request that was temporarily reinforced by two of his chiefs coming up, seizing him by the arms and making him sit down. The old man seemed, said Phillips, 'dejected and frightened'.

From here on the accounts of what immediately followed become confused. There were numerous people who claim to have been eye-witnesses and it is not suggested for a moment that any one of them lied or gave a distorted account or tried to show himself in the best light. As mentioned earlier in this book, when an action is as sudden and as brief as it is violent, no two accounts ever agree.

What is certain is that there were two to three thousand

natives clustered around Cook. Phillips asked if he should draw the marines up by the water's edge and to this Cook apparently agreed – although this left him isolated and unprotected. Then shots were heard further along the beach and the report came in that an important chief, trying to leave the shore without authorisation, had been killed. This was, unfortunately, true and inflamed the mob. A man with a pahua – a sharp-pointed bar of iron about two feet long- approached Cook threateningly, pahua in one hand, his war mat – a shield – in the other. Cook fired, either a blank or small shot which did not penetrate the mat, and at once fierce fighting broke out. Both the marines on shore and those some way out in the boats discharged volleys and Cook himself killed a man. Soon the fighting was hand to hand, bayonets and butts against clubs and pahuas. As they were so hopelessly outnumbered, it was obvious that the marines could last moments only.

It was said of Cook that, because of the awe in which the Hawaiians still held him, they would not touch him as long as he faced them, but as he turned to wave the boats to come in, he was struck down by a club. It is significant, perhaps, that the wielder of the club was Koa, the high priest. Within seconds, dozens of others had fallen upon Cook, now lying in shallow water, and stabbed him with their knives and pahuas time and time and time again. The time was 8 a.m. He was fifty years old.

The grief-maddened crews begged of Captain Clerke that they be allowed to take their revenge. Clerke, a man clearly possessed of as much wisdom as he was of force of character, refused: he was well aware that if such permission were given reprisals would be on so massive a scale that they would not cease while there was one Hawaiian left alive in Kealakekua Bay. Clerke did not believe that there was any degree of premeditation about the affair: Cook having the nature he did and the natives having the natures they had, he regarded it as inevitable that it could not have ended in any other way.

Cook's remains were buried at sea on 22 February. Clerke, who was mortally ill, should have taken the expedition home but as a tribute to 'my good friend Captain Cook' he took the *Resolution* and *Discovery* through the Bering Strait and into the Arctic again: but he had no more success than Cook had had the previous summer. Clerke died on the way back to England where the *Resolution* and the *Discovery* arrived on 4 October 1780, four years and three months after Cook had set out on his last voyage.

Epilogue

AND so, shabbily, shockingly, violently, a great man came to his end. There is, almost, a certain fitness, a certain inevitable element of Greek tragedy in that he was to die when he did, at the height of his powers and his fame. He had achieved, it is very likely, all he was ever destined to achieve, for his last great task was an impossible one: we know now that there is no North-West Passage and that if you want to make your own you take a nuclear-powered ice-breaker along with you.

For what would Cook have done next? It is impossible to see that, in terms of the life he had been leading since he had set out on his first great voyage twelve years previously, Cook could have had any future. Of course, there were still places to be explored, surveyed, charted. But what kind of places? When the world has been a man's oyster, when he has used it as a child uses his back yard, you do not send that man to poke around in little pockets of exploratory resistance, pockets that exist within the overall context of the already known. For Cook, the only challenge was the *unknown* – or nothing. And who can believe that this man whose questing spirit had taken him where man had never been before would have been content to rusticate and decline within the narrow confines of Greenwich Hospital? For this man, with his titanic achievements behind him, had no worlds left to conquer, no place left to go: perhaps the gods were kind and struck him down.

No one will ever strike his fame down. Cook's place in history is secure. That would please him for that means that mankind recognises the greatness of the achievements of a man for whom achievement meant all.

The incomparable determination, persistence and re-solution he showed until a set goal was achieved was as clearly recognised then as it is now and those qualities figure prominently in the farewell tributes paid him by two of his contemporaries who knew him among the best of all.

Samwell, surgeon's mate on the *Resolution* for Cook's last voyage wrote:

Nature had endowed him with a mind vigorous and com-prehensive, which in his riper years he had cultivated with care and industry. His general knowledge was extensive and various: in that of his own profession he was unequalled. With a clear judg-ment, strong masculine sense, and the most determined resolution: with a genius peculiarly turned for enterprise, he pursued his object with unshaken perseverance – vigilant and active in an eminent degree: cool and intrepid among dangers: patient and firm under difficulties and distress: fertile in expedients: great and original in all his designs: active and resolved in carrying them into execution. In every situation he stood unrivalled and alone: on him all eyes were turned: he was our leading star, which at its setting left us involved in darkness and despair.

Sir Hugh Palliser, Comptroller of the Navy, Cook's friend and colleague over many years and the man who was the very first to recognise Cook's latent genius, erected a memorial in his own estate at Chalfont St Giles, Buckingham-shire: it echoes Samwell's words:

He raised himself, solely by his merit from a very obscure birth, to the rank of Post Captain in the royal navy, and was unfortunately killed by the Savages of the island of Owhyhee [Hawaii], on the 14th of February 1779; which island he had not long before discovered, when prosecuting his third voyage round the globe.

He possessed, in an eminent degree, all the qualifications requisite for his profession and great undertakings; together with the amiable and worthy qualities of the best men. Cool and deliberate in judging: sagacious in determining: active in execu-ting: steady and persevering in enterprising from vigilance and unremitting caution: unsubdued by labour, difficulties, and disappointments, fertile in expedients: never wanting presence of mind: always possessing himself and the full use of a sound understanding.

'I, who had ambition not only to go farther than anyone had done before, but as far as it was possible for man to go . . .'

The monument to Cook erected by Sir Hugh Palliser at Vache
Park, Buckinghamshire

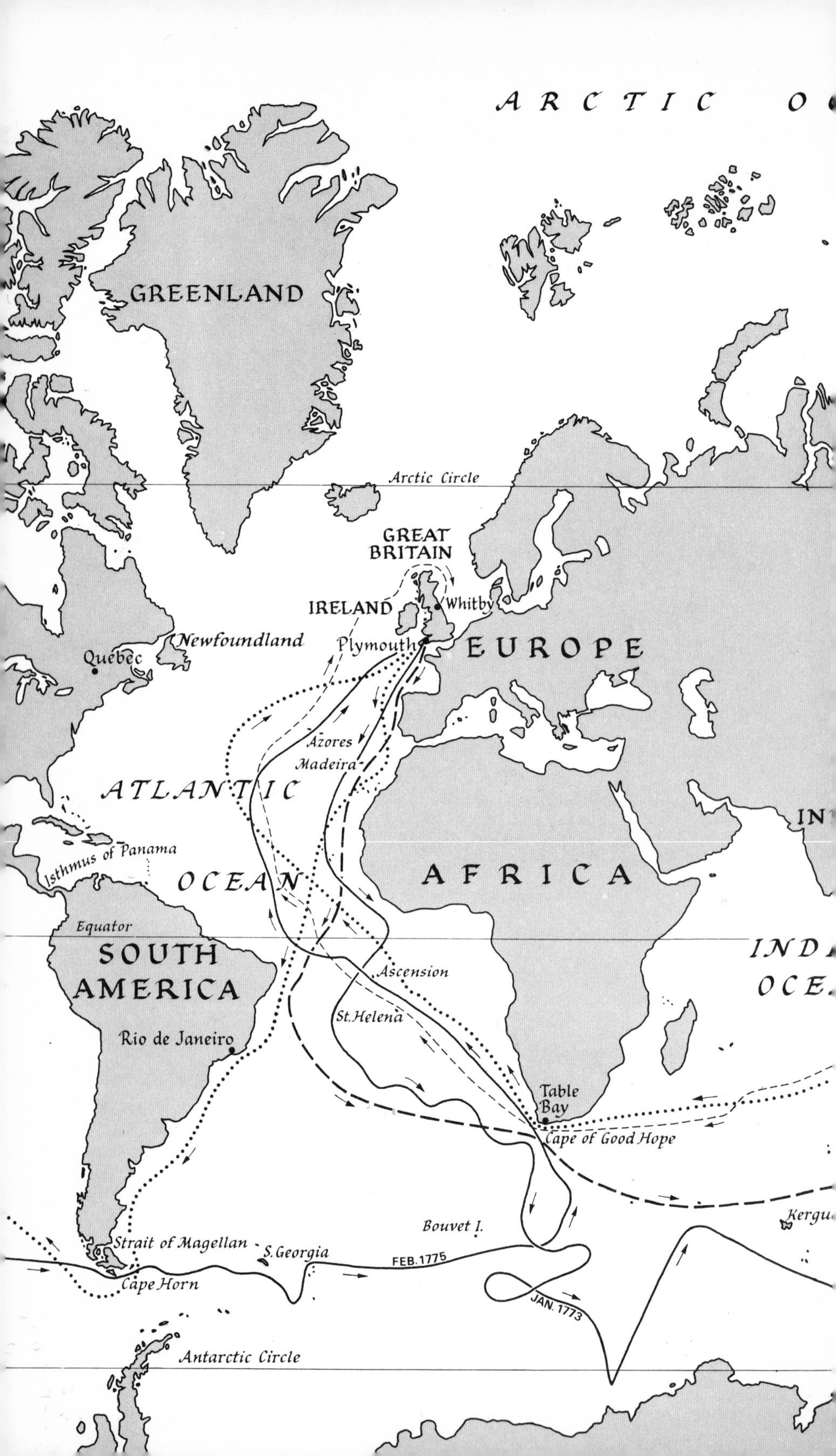

ARCTIC O

GREENLAND

Arctic Circle

GREAT
BRITAIN

IRELAND   Whitby

Newfoundland   Plymouth   EUROPE

Québec

Azores
Madeira

ATLANTIC

Isthmus of Panama

OCEAN   AFRICA   IN

Equator

SOUTH
AMERICA   Ascension

Rio de Janeiro   St. Helena

Table
Bay

Cape of Good Hope

Bouvet I.   Kergu

Strait of Magellan   S. Georgia   FEB. 1775

Cape Horn   JAN. 1773

Antarctic Circle

MAP OF COOK'S THREE VOYAGES

.... *First Voyage*
       1768~1771

———— *Second Voyage*
       1772~1775

— — — *Third Voyage*
       1776~1779

- - - - - *Homeward Voyage*
       of Cook's Crew

Bering Strait

ASIA

ALASKA

Cook Inlet

NORTH AMERICA

Kamchatka
Petropavlovsk

Aleutian Is.

Unalaska

Prince
William
Sound

MAY 1778

OCT. 1778

Nootka
Sound

JAPAN

P A C I F I C

FEB. 1778

NA

APR. 1779

NOV. 1779

Macao

Hawaiian Is.

Philippine
Islands
Mactan

Guam

Marshall Is.

O C E A N

Caroline Is.

BORNEO

NEW GUINEA

Gilbert Is.

Christmas I.

Batavia   Moluccas
Java

Solomon
Islands

Marquesas Is.

New
Hebrides

Fiji Is.

Society
Is.

AUSTRALIA

Great Barrier Reef

New
Caledonia
OCT.
1774

Friendly
Is.

Cook Is.

Tahiti

Easter I.

OCT.
1773

FEB. 1774

Botany
Bay

Tasmania

JULY 1773

NEW
ZEALAND

NOV. 1774

DEC. 1773

Acknowledgments

Bildarchiv der Österreichische Nationalbibliothek, Vienna 108; reproduced by kind permission of the Earl of Birkenhead, 105; Trustees of the British Museum, **frontispiece**, **1**, **2**, **19**, 6, 23, 28, 45, 50, 52/3, 55, 62, 64, 66, 66/7, 80, 84/5, 92/3, 97, 101, 114/5, 133, 136/7, 140/1, 144, 145, 158, 159, 176; by permission of the Trustees of the British Museum (Natural History), **15**, **16**, 40, 41, 47, 70, 78, 83, 87, 110, 111, 128; High Commissioner for New Zealand 184; reproduced by kind permission of George Howard, Esq., **18**; Mitchell Library, Sydney, **10**, **14**, 26; National Library of Australia, Canberra, **20/21**, 32/3, 122; National Maritime Museum, Greenwich, **7**, 16, 22, 30, 34, 75, 160/1, 166, 167 (on loan from the Ministry of Defence, Navy), **3**, **4/5**, **8/9**, **12/13**, **17**, 112, 125, 154/5, 168/9, 172/3 (Greenwich Hospital Collection), 19, 151; Public Record Office, London, 35; Science Museum, London (Crown Copyright), 58, 164 (on loan from the Royal Society), 38; Whitby Literary and Philosophical Society, 14; Historisches Museum, Berne, 163; from the Collection at Parkham Park, Sussex, **6**; reproduced by authority of the Ministry of Defence, **11**; Mr and Mrs Rienits Collection, London, **22**.

Photographs: Derek Bayes 12, 25; Blinkhorn-Haynes 105; R. B. Fleming & Co. **15**, 28, 40, 47, 70, 78, 83, 92/3, 110, 111, 128; Peter Parkinson 23; Tindale's 14; Eileen Tweedy **11**, **16**, **18**, 6, 22, 52/3, 97, 114/5, 133, 136/7, 140/1, 144, 145; Science Museum, London 102/3; Axel Poignant, **6** (below); Michael Holford, **22**.
The model of the *Endeavour* illustrated on page 34 was made by craftsmen at the National Maritime Museum and was presented to the New Zealand Government by the British Government.

Index

INDEX

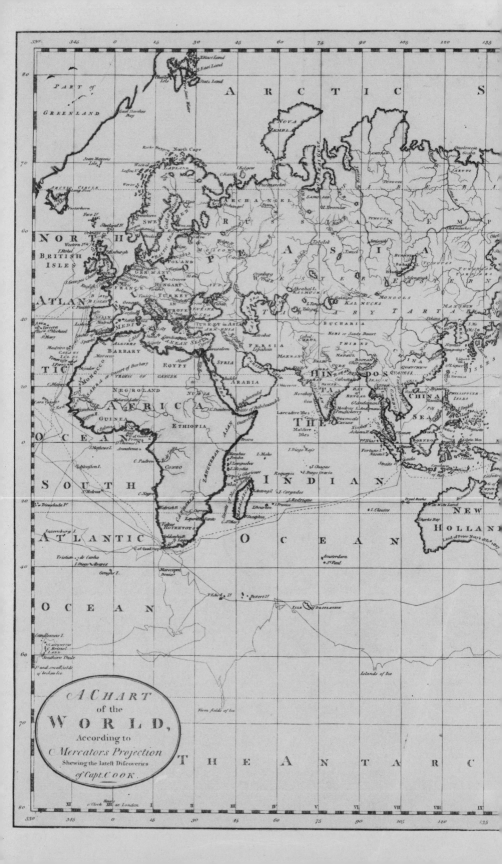

A CHART
of the
WORLD,
According to
Mercators Projection
Shewing the latest Discoveries
of Capt. COOK.